CONVERSATIONS WITH COGGAN

Also by Robin Daniels

Blackpool Football: the Official Club History (Hale, 1972)
Conversations with Cardus (Gollancz, 1976)
Conversations with Menuhin (Macdonald, 1979)

CONVERSATIONS WITH COGGAN

Robin Daniels

Foreword by Cardinal Basil Hume

HODDER AND STOUGHTON
LONDON SYDNEY AUCKLAND TORONTO

ACKNOWLEDGEMENTS

I am most grateful to Cardinal Hume for contributing the Foreword for this book. This is an especially tangible expression of his friendship with Lord Coggan for it was written during the time of preparation for the Pope's 1982 visit to Britain.

I am grateful to Lady Coggan; the Very Reverend Edward Carpenter, Dean of Westminster; Prebendary D. W. Cleverley Ford, formerly Senior Chaplain to Lord Coggan; Rev. Harry Snape; Kate and Russell Dore; Barbara Lepper; John Marsh; Joseph Ingram; Hilary Mousley; Mary Cryer, Lambeth Palace secretary; Anne Nellist; John Miles and Jackie Turner of the Church Information Office.

I owe much to Rob Warner, my editor at Hodders, and to his secretary, Louise Tulip. Both have given me all possible guidance and support.

The late William Narraway's painting of Lord Coggan was photographed at Lambeth Palace by John R. Rifkin. It is reproduced on the dust jacket of this book by kind permission of the Archbishop of Canterbury and the Church Commissioners.

Unless stated otherwise, all Biblical quotations are from the Authorised Version.

R. D.

British Library Cataloguing in Publication Data
Daniels, Robin
  Conversations with Coggan
  1. Coggan, Donald   2. Church of England—Biography
  I. Title   II. Coggan, Donald
  283'.092'4   BX5199.C/

ISBN 0 340 32638 7

Hodder and Stoughton Editorial Office: 47 Bedford Square, London WC1B 3DP.

With thanks for much love and understanding, I dedicate this book to my father, to my aunt and uncle (Kate and Russell Dore), to Aileen Follett, Sister Nora Lucilla C.S.P., Kathleen and Eric Watkins, also to those now departed this life—my mother, and the Rev. Arthur Bray and his wife Muriel.

R. D.

Robin Daniels is a writer, occasionally a speaker on radio, and a psychotherapist in private practice. He has trained in both the Freudian and Jungian schools of psychoanalysis.

Robin Daniels was born in Blackpool in 1941, of Anglo-American parentage. He was educated in California and at Epsom College and later studied music with Alan Rowlands.

Before entering the caring professions in 1972, he was, in turn, a wool broker, music critic, work-study engineer, new-products designer, and fund-raiser for the Spastics Society.

His books have been well received by press and public. His first book, *Blackpool Football*, was voted one of the best sports books of the year by BBC Radio's *Sport on 2*. *Conversations with Menuhin* was a choice of Readers' Union, Britain's longest-established book club.

Conversations with Cardus was one of the *Sunday Times*'s books of the year, and Dennis Silk ended his *Sunday Telegraph* review with these words, 'If you want to learn about the art of living, read this book.'

CONTENTS

ILLUSTRATIONS

Between pages 80–81

FOREWORD

I am pleased to contribute a foreword to this book of 'Conversations'. As Donald Coggan says, he and I have been 'close friends and colleagues in Christ' for many years.

Written in a relatively informal way, this book is essentially autobiographical in nature. It imparts, almost casually, many of Lord Coggan's deeply-held beliefs and hopes, thoughts and attitudes, fears and views, along with many interesting details about the events of his life, not least his very happy family life.

From a somewhat sheltered home, he moved through public school, Cambridge, and a lectureship in Manchester University, before embracing Anglican orders, which, however, had been his ultimate goal since boyhood. He describes his life thereafter as 'an adventure of faith' in which he went from a curacy in Islington, via a spell of teaching in Canada, to principalship of the London College of Divinity, and to the episcopate. He looks back affectionately and gratefully to his nineteen years in the North of England, first as Bishop of Bradford and later as Archbishop of York. It was in this period that he and I first had contact with each other. It was from York in 1974 that he was translated to the See of Canterbury.

Lord Coggan describes his life as Anglican Primate as a time in which he 'almost lurched from one activity to another, moved on by the impetus of events'. This may be how it felt to him, but it is obvious from other comments and reflections that he brought great deliberation and consultation to all the major decisions and problems of his time at Canterbury, as well as the considerable scholarship and concern for accuracy in detail which is equally obvious throughout this volume.

I hope that in his retirement he may find it possible to continue some form of creative work and of work with people, for, as he says himself, 'What more can a man ask?'

I am happy to welcome Robin Daniels's book about Donald Coggan. Although we do not agree on all matters of doctrine, yet I know that we are close to each other in our shared striving to love the same Lord.

Basil Hume

APRIL, 1982   CARDINAL ARCHBISHOP OF WESTMINSTER

INTRODUCTION

This book was born in a week of contrasts. In March 1980, Robert Runcie was enthroned as Archbishop of Canterbury. Leaders—royal, political, religious—from Europe, the Far East, every continent, attended this centuries-old service and, joining forces, sang to the music of a great Cathedral's organ and a glorious choir.

Four days later I was the only passenger to alight from the train at a dwarf of a station in Kent. There, for the first time, I met Donald Coggan. Tradition had prevented his being at the enthronement of his successor; instead Lord Coggan had watched the ceremony on television.

As I got into the car he said he hoped our meeting didn't mean my missing the Grand National—an event which on this day was far from my thoughts. My mother had died a few weeks previously, and Donald Coggan's parting words were a promise to pray for me and my father during Easter. Such was the range of our first encounter.

He and his wife, Jean, only two months after their move, seemed already very much at home. We sat in his study, with its low, period ceiling, its shelves of books, and a red candle.

In his last eighteen months as Archbishop of Canterbury, he had travelled to Canada and the United States, to Scandinavia, West Africa, East Germany and Hungary, and to Rome for the Inauguration of Pope John Paul II. Donald Coggan's base, no longer Lambeth Palace, was now a cottage in a tiny village, with no secretary to help him answer letters and invitations from all over the world.

I soon realised that, for him, retirement would mean no real let-up in his activity: soon he would be in the United States to preach and lecture; he was planning a visit to the Far East later in the year; a London publisher had invited him to write a life of Saint Paul; and he would speak in the House of Lords 'on

11

any issue I felt strongly about, such as education and any Bill closely affecting the well-being of family life—moral issues'.

I sensed in him a rare combination of gentleness and strength: modest strength; harnessed energy. He compels respect because he has natural authority: the authority of a man who has read widely, thought deeply, and travelled far; a man for whom prayer and witness are central and essential.

He is grateful each day for Jean's love, comfort, and companionship. 'We think we must have first seen each other from a pram! We were both taken to Frinton and may have been there in the same summer. Later the influence of the Children's Special Service Mission was strong, thanks to young students, full of love for the Lord, who wanted to pass on this love to others.' After forty-seven years of married life he can still say with sincerity, 'Even if we are apart for only a few hours, when we are together again we have such a lot to share.'

He is a man who cares. I always come away from a meeting with new learning, more faith, a benediction, and the certainty of continuous contact, in mind and in spirit.

He is a man of humility. He speaks objectively and without pride of when he was 'York and later Canterbury'. And the day before he was due to preach on John 14:6—'I am the way, the truth, and the life'—he said, 'This is a big subject for a small man.'

He is both a serious scholar and a man of humour. On a shelf in his study, alongside heavyweight theology and biography, is *The Complete Book of Limericks*.

One day I quoted to him a Gallup Poll finding—from a month before he left Canterbury—showing ever-increasing belief in God with the advance of years. Belief in God, in Heaven, and in an after-life, all tend to increase with each decade of life. 'Perhaps,' mused Donald Coggan, 'this is because older people are anxiously studying for their finals!'

LONDON, FEBRUARY 1982   ROBIN DANIELS

God is always to be found in the present moment.
(from the conversation on High Office)

1 ORIGINS

R.D. When did you have your first intimation that you might one day become a priest?

D.C. My vocation was clear enough when I was about sixteen to make me change course in midstream. If I could see a transcript of what was going on in my mind in those teenage years, I'm sure I'd see the influence of the man who prepared me for confirmation in 1925, Gladstone Sargent, a young and lively incumbent.

My wife's maternal grandfather was Rector of Palgrave, Norfolk, but being in the priesthood is not part of my family's traditions. My father was a business-man in London, and it was with fear and trembling that I told him I wanted to switch subjects at school.

I went to Merchant Taylors' School rather late, at fourteen, and my father entered me on what was called the 'modern side', with the focus on French and German and a bit of science.

Then, at the age of sixteen, I changed subjects and started learning Greek and Hebrew: it was my good fortune that Merchant Taylors' was one of the few public schools where Hebrew was taught. And in my few remaining terms at public school I had to prepare for university entrance. This was quite a traumatic change, and it put me under increased pressure both at home and at school, but my conviction, my desire to enter the ministry of the Church, must have been strong enough by then to enable me to face this new challenge. I had been, so far as a youngster can be, a committed Christian well before that time. During the period when I was attending a small preparatory school in Burnham-on-Sea, Somerset, I used to worship with my mother and my sisters at our local parish church.

R.D. What was there about Gladstone Sargent that was speaking to you very deeply?

D.C. He had a most attractive and sunny personality, and he loved young people. He was musical—on his piano he used to play to me choruses he had composed—and his preaching gripped me. So I thought to myself, 'How marvellous to be able to spend one's life in this way.'

At around this time, or perhaps a little bit later, I came to see something of what work in slum areas was like. Those were the days, in the middle or late Twenties, before the advent of the Welfare State: ramshackle housing, overcrowding, scant provision for sickness, the general effects of unemployment, children's toes poking out of the fronts of their boots.

I saw all this at first hand in Hoxton, then one of the roughest areas in London. During school and college holidays I used to go to a Christian mission in the very centre of Hoxton, and there I'd do my best to assist a little old man by the name of Lewis Burt. He was not a priest—I don't know what his religious affiliation was—but he was deeply concerned for the welfare of these people who were living in appalling conditions.

Lewis Burt was an engaging personality, a Cockney with a scraggy moustache and with a bowler hat perched on the back of his head. One day, while we walked through the streets of Hoxton, he stopped for a few minutes to join some children in a game they were playing. As we left, he beamed and said, stressing every word, 'Workers together with God!' Thus did Lewis Burt cast glory on the ordinary.

This was the kind of work I wanted to devote my life to. I began to see myself, my future, as a priest, perhaps in an East End parish. Things worked out rather differently, but those were my thoughts at that time.

R.D. Did you have any earlier boyhood ambitions?

D.C. Not that I can recall. I don't think I had any idea where I was going until my change of course at school.

A few years later (1931), when I was in my last year at

16

Cambridge and coming up for part two of the Tripos in Oriental Languages, I was intending to go straight on to theological college. But one day the Chaplain of St. John's College, J. S. Boys Smith, who later became Master of the College and Vice-chancellor of the University, left a note in my room asking me to go and see him. He told me of a post at Manchester University for an assistant lecturer in Semitic Languages and Literature, and suggested that I might consider applying. I did and was accepted. This was not another change of direction; only a short postponement. I taught at the University for three years, and they wanted to reappoint me for another three. But having gained this extra training and experience, I now wanted to go straight for my goal— ordination.

I have never regretted my years at Manchester. They helped to broaden my touch with life before going into the ministry. They also gave me the opportunity of seeing a first-class modern university after taking my degree at an ancient one.

R.D.   And in those inter-war years Manchester was a thriving centre of culture.

D.C.   Yes, I was living for the first time in the north of England, in a city famous not only for its trade but also for that great editor C. P. Scott and the *Manchester Guardian*, for the Hallé Orchestra, for its libraries. Manchester was a most stimulating place to live in and to experience in my last years as a layman.

And it was a university of real distinction. I overlapped for a short period with C. H. Dodd before he went to take up the Norris-Hulse Chair of Divinity at Cambridge. He had brought many qualities to what was already a distinguished Chair of Biblical Studies at Manchester. There was also a fine school of history and an equally fine school of philosophy. The Vice-Chancellor during my years there was Walter Moberly, a member of a family of distinguished writers and theologians. Sir Walter's father, Dr. R. C. Moberly, held several senior appointments at Oxford—he was for a time Canon of Christ Church—and wrote many important books. Two are worthy of special mention: *Atonement and Personality*, and *Ministerial Priesthood* which was published in 1897 and reissued in 1969.

Manchester gave me my first experience of teaching. You weren't taught how to lecture; you were just thrown in at the deep end. You learned how to arrange your material, and you had to prepare carefully so as to be able to respond to questions. All this was invaluable training for what turned out to be my work in later years.

R.D. As you look back, can you describe how your lecture style developed? For example, how did you manage to set up a dialogue with young people, some of whom were probably unsure of their ground?

D.C. At Manchester the classes were quite small, most of them, so it was easy for the students to participate. Sometimes, for one of the more esoteric topics, a class—or seminar as it would be called today—might consist of only two or three students.

An introductory Hebrew class would be larger, perhaps as many as twenty, because of the many students from different denominations of the Church in Manchester, which was quite a centre for theological education.

Later on, when teaching in Toronto and at the London College of Divinity, the classes were also reasonably small, so I could often pause for questions. And when teaching from a text, Hebrew or Greek, I would ask the students in turn to render a passage into English to see how they were getting on. So the atmosphere was shared and intimate.

Whether this teaching affected my preaching style, I'm not sure. A preacher varies his style according to the size and intellect of the congregation. For example, if I am in a small church my preaching is more conversational than when I am in a cathedral.

R.D. Going back as far as you can remember, to your first experiences of church-going, can you recall any particular preacher who so inspired you that you said to yourself, 'I'd love to go into a pulpit and preach'?

D.C. My memory fades a bit as I try to go back as far as that, but I'm sure I heard some good sermons in the mid–Twenties, my years at public school, when our family used to attend services at St. Peter's, Highgate. E. G. A. Dunn, a wonderful man and priest, was Vicar of St. Peter's from 1911–23. He gave me a fine example of Christ's ministry in action. Dunn was followed by Gladstone Sargent, who prepared me for confirmation.

R.D. Was there a Christian Union at Merchant Taylors', a small fellowship of friends you could rely on during some of the hardships of public-school life?

D.C. Yes, there was a small Christian Union, and I helped with the organising of our meetings. We used to invite speakers, people such as the evangelist Canon Bryan Green, who was an old Merchant Taylor. Sometimes we were laughed at for our faith, but I'm sure this had a strengthening effect.

R.D. Going back to early home life, how did you spend your leisure time?

D.C. I was very keen on playing the piano and passed the various grades of the Royal College exams. A marvellous little man, Professor Koch, used to teach me. And then I became interested in organ-playing.

When I was very young, Mother used to read to me and my sisters: at this time I came to love Dickens and Scott. School prizes I won included Pepys's *Diary* and the collected works of Shakespeare; and my father used to bring me books from a red-covered series of English classics, each costing two shillings.

R.D. You had quite a long spell of poor health, didn't you, before going to Merchant Taylors'.

D.C. Yes, and I had to have my lessons at home. My tutor was a widow, Helen Gardner, who was helping her family finances by teaching. When our family went to St. Anne's, Brookfield, at the bottom of Highgate Hill, she would be there with her children. One of them is now Dame Helen Gardner,

Emeritus Professor of English Literature at Oxford. Her mother gave me a good grounding, especially on the arts side.

R.D. How did your parents respond when you told them you wanted to be ordained?

D.C. My mother was delighted. I shouldn't think there was a tremor of doubt in her mind. In her own quiet way, she was a deeply religious woman, a fine Christian. Telling my father—as I've said—was quite a thing. He took the news well, to my immense relief, and never complained or took issue with me. This was a sign of grace on his part, for he had pictured me as working in the City. Having faced the fact that my mind was made up, he never stood in my way. And though he said very little in the years that followed, I have a feeling that in his own reserved way he was proud of any successes—as he would have regarded them—that came my way. It was natural for a City business-man to be ambitious for his son and to think in terms of 'promotion' and 'arriving'.

R.D. You said he was a business-man. What kind of work did he do?

D.C. He was a director and the company secretary of a group of butchers' shops, Lidstone's. That was his life-work. You still see the name here and there, especially in North London.

He was a churchwarden at St. Martin's, Gospel Oak, and was a close friend of the Vicar, T. H. Russell. One day my father said, 'Donald, I've got a present for you.' I wondered what was coming. 'I've paid for you to have sixty organ lessons.'

That was a splendid and well-timed gift. It was given to me when I was making the switch from modern languages to classics, those two crucial years, at seventeen and eighteen, when I was preparing for Cambridge and working very intensely. Once a week, on my half-day off, I used to go to St. Martin's for an organ lesson given by Mr. Gibbons. I often played at church services and even gave a recital once. I tremble to think of it!

20

On the other hand, I'm glad to recall the day my father came home with a Greek Testament for me. He was kind in his own quiet way, offering little signs of support now and then, but he was a very silent man.

My father was a self-contained man. He spent very little time at home. He was out at work all day and usually came home late at night. The rest of the family didn't see much of him. He didn't even come on summer holidays with us. He would come and say goodbye to us at the station and give each of us a crisp new ten-shilling note, which was a fortune for a youngster in those days. But we never got to know him in any depth. In fact we were rather frightened of him.

Mother was a wonderful person, a saint. She was a deeply religious person. She didn't say much about her faith but it *shone*.

She had a restricted married life. Looking back, we had extraordinarily little social life, which was a great loss for me and my sisters. It made me very shy and meant that I didn't become a normal social being until much later in life.

R.D. With your father not being at home for so much of the time, which of your parents was responsible for discipline?

D.C. I suppose Mother was, but I never think of her as being a disciplinarian: I would have felt so awful if I had done anything to cause her any distress. I was rather frightened of Father, not that he ever beat us.

R.D. Were you influenced by your mother's religious nature?

D.C. Yes, in our young days we were encouraged to take part in the activities of the Children's Special Service Mission. These missions were held in seaside towns all over the country. Undergraduates, in their college blazers, accompanied by their girlfriends, would build a giant sand-castle as a focal point to attract young children. We'd have an informal religious service in the morning, and beach games, treasure hunts, discussions and a whole range of activities all through the day. Everyone gained benefit: the organisers themselves, the parents and the children. We received and absorbed the Christian message in a joyful and spontaneous way. Many priests and active lay people owe much to the early influence of the C.S.S.M. For example, Max Warren described in his autobiography *Crowded Canvas* how the C.S.S.M. not only brought religion alive for him for the first time but also gave him priceless experience of leadership, team-work, public speaking and, most of all, lasting friendships.

Later, in my university days, I was Treasurer and Vice-President of the Cambridge Inter-Collegiate Christian Union. My early roots in Christian life may have been somewhat conservative, but those roots had depth and a strong Biblical basis. In later years I hope I have broadened and developed, and come to see implications in the faith which at one time I could only glimpse.

The kind of person my mother was must have spoken to me much louder than what she said. She made a vivid and lasting impression on me, without ever trying to expound the Creed to me. And when she knelt to pray, to lead family prayers, she was more likely to make use of a book of prayers than offer prayers of her own invention.

R.D.   How long did your parents live?

D.C.   My mother died, bless her, in 1938, just after we got to Canada. My father married again and died a few years later. I came back to England, after my mother died, to see him and my sisters. I got to know my father a bit better on that visit but never saw him again.

R.D.   Your grandfathers—what kind of work did they do?

D.C.   My father's father, William Coggan, worked for that same company of butchers. I remember him well: a big, kindly, bearded man, with a rather forbidding wife. Grandma was stern, a martinet. My father was one of seven brothers who filled a couple of pews in Dulwich Church, Sunday by Sunday.

R.D.   And on your mother's side?

D.C.   Her father was what in those days was called a 'gentleman farmer'. Think how people would react these days if you used such a snobbish description: it implied that the other farmers were not quite gentlemen!

They lived in the West Country, and my mother was born in Taunton, Somerset. My father brought his young bride to London around the turn of the century and they lived on Croftdown Road at the bottom of Highgate Hill, just over the tramlines from the entrance to Parliament Hill Fields. It was a lovely area.

R.D. Have you, or any member of your family, done any delving into your family history?

D.C. Yes, my elder sister has done some research. So far as I know, Coggan is an Irish name. My mother and father decided to do me proud: I was named Frederick for England, Donald for Scotland, and Coggan for Ireland!

R.D. You have two sisters . . .

D.C. Yes, both older than I am: Norah by seven years, and Beatrice by three or four. So I was the baby of the family, and the only boy.

R.D. I'd be glad if you would tell me a bit about them.

D.C. They both lead interesting lives. Norah has been a parish worker in Birmingham and in other places, including Sevenoaks where she now lives. And she was Central Secretary of the Ladies' Home Mission Union, later to become known as Women's Action, a society which trains and finances women lay workers in the Church. Neither of my sisters married.

The younger one, Beatrice—or Trixy, as she is called—didn't begin her nurse's training until relatively late in life. This is because Mother was in fragile health. Trixy cared for her until she died early in 1938, just after my wife, Jean, and I had arrived in Canada. After training at St. Mary's Hospital during the war, Trixy worked for many years for the Church Missionary Society, in the Near East and in Africa. Then she became matron of a home for old people here in England. Now she has retired and lives in a flat in Richmond and rebukes us all by the number of good works she still manages to accomplish. She is a most unselfish person. I always tell her that if entry into heaven were gained by good works—which it certainly is not!—she would be luxuriating in a front seat while I, if I were allowed in at all, would be crawling about at the rear!

R.D.   When you were in your teens, were you close enough to your sisters to ask for their reaction to your vocation?

D.C.   I don't remember asking them, but I am sure they were both wholeheartedly in favour.

R.D.   At this crucial time in your life was there anyone, in your family or perhaps at school, with whom you had enough rapport to be able to say, 'This is what I really want to do. You know me quite well. How does it sound to you?'

D.C.   I didn't ask any family friends; in fact my parents seldom invited people to visit our home.

One of my closest friends was John Pendlebury. He followed his father into bank work and was later ordained. He was killed in his bed by a bomb during the last war. I'm sure I received great encouragement from John and my other friends at school, some of whom, like me, were committed Christians.

I was helped and inspired by the Reverend F. J. Padfield, who was my Hebrew master at Merchant Taylors'. He was a charming person with a lovely sense of humour. He imbued in me a great love for the study of Hebrew. His was a welcome and timely influence on a boy whose mind was just beginning to open. I was a late developer. Not until I was about sixteen did my intellect really begin to function: I began to get a feel for languages and I saw for the first time what fun scholarship could be. No member of my family inspired my love of languages; nor had I been especially keen on French and German. Discovering my aptitude for Hebrew opened up for me the whole realm of learning: what came alive for me, in those teenage years, has never ceased to fascinate me. At last I had found a subject I could enjoy and do well at. Before then I had lacked confidence in myself and suffered from feelings of inferiority. I owe quite a lot to Padfield. He lit the lamp of scholarship in me at that very crucial age.

I had been held back by poor health at a time when—especially in a public school—to excel at sport was the main way to win popularity. Also, I lacked experience of meeting people, for we had very few visitors at home. My discovery of music and of Hebrew, and later the support of a loving wife, all came as a revelation to me. Romans (5:3–5) has a most helpful comment on this: '. . . we glory in tribulations also: knowing that tribulation worketh patience; and patience, experience; and experience, hope . . . because the love of God is shed abroad in our hearts by the Holy Ghost which is given unto us.'

I think also, down the years, of Spencer Leeson, who became headmaster at Merchant Taylors' a year or two before I left. Even in that short time I could see the impact he was making on the school. A young headmaster, he gave a fresh and energetic tone to the whole of school life, with renewed emphasis on extra-curricular activities, music and hobbies. I can hear Leeson now, with his terrible stutter, lecturing to us in the Hebrew room on the Maccabees: when he began a sentence he would rise on the balls of his feet and then, having at last squeezed out the words, sink back on his heels with relief.

He went on to be Headmaster of Winchester, and then he was ordained deacon and priest and made Prebendary—all in about a year. He went to St. Mary's, Southampton, and then became Bishop of Peterborough. One year at Oxford he gave the Bampton Divinity Lectures. Leeson, large of mind and personality, with a love of beauty, music, art, and all the good things of life, was one of the men who shaped and broadened me.

2 PREPARATION

R.D. You worked for a few years in Islington, in the mid-Thirties, a time when there were many unemployed and no welfare state. Did that period, albeit short, influence you after the war, in the way you saw social issues and the needs of the individual?

D.C. Yes, I'm sure you are right. I was in Islington for nearly three years, first as junior then as senior curate. I was ordained deacon in September 1934 and priest in 1935 in St. Paul's Cathedral, and soon after that Jean and I were married.

During part of my time in Islington the Vicar, J. M. Hewitt, was away because of his mother's death and for other reasons, so I had considerable responsibilities for a young man in a large parish.

I had grown up with rather an individualistic faith, and with very little social awareness. Now in my twenties, within a stone's throw of my church, I saw a family of fourteen living in two rooms. They had no bathroom, and what they used for beds were stacked in the living-room during the day and laid out at night. I was now suddenly and fully exposed to the realities of poverty, unemployment and inadequate housing, and this had a profound effect on me.

Hitherto, I had gone from a rather sheltered home to public school, to Cambridge, and then to Manchester University as a young don. There I took great interest in the work of the Manchester City Mission. I was a member of the Board, and on Sunday nights I often preached at Mission meetings in run-down areas of Manchester and Salford: an enlightening contrast for me after the intensity of university life and work during the week. That period, together with the visits I had paid to Hoxton a few years earlier, meant that I was not unaware of social conditions different from my own

26

upbringing. But as a curate I was seeing them every day, *in medias res*, and I am very grateful for that experience.

R.D. As you look back on your life, did you ever have an experience of deprivation: suffering temporary loss of health; or not attaining a major ambition; or being without enough money?

D.C. I have never been short of money to the point of deprivation, but our family was by no means rich. I never knew much about my father's business affairs but, looking back, I suspect he had at least one hard patch. To supplement the scholarship I was awarded when I went to Cambridge, I was given various grants: presumably this was because of my family's financial needs.

As for health, I suffered very badly from asthma for many years. As a small boy, I had a delicate constitution. In my earlier school years—during the First World War when I was at prep school in Burnham-on-Sea and indeed after that—my asthma was so bad that I couldn't participate in sport, and I used to dread having to go up a long flight of stairs.

But the outcome of the asthma was more painful than the asthma itself. In the twenties I went to a public school of an old-fashioned type, with an old-fashioned headmaster. To be unable to take part in sport or in the Officers' Training Corps made me a pariah, and this bit into my soul more than physical suffering affected my body.

R.D. Did your contemporaries at school make life difficult?

D.C. Yes, very difficult. I was bullied in my early days at Merchant Taylors', and to a sensitive teenage boy this was painful. As a Christian, I tried to resist the temptation to fight back. Later on, I was forced to stand up for myself: for me, this was a real transformation.

I can only hope that those years made me more responsive to the suffering of others.

R.D. And the asthma—did that clear up later?

D.C. Yes, it may well have been mainly psychosomatic. For a long time I went to a very fine American osteopath,

Mr. Dunning, who had a practice in London. He helped me enormously. Between sixteen and eighteen I at last began to find life a bit easier, thanks to the osteopath and to my studies, which were of ever-more-absorbing interest.

R.D.   How wonderful that a few years before you entered the Ministry, in which a good speaking voice is so important, the asthma was lifted from you.

D.C.   Yes, since being ordained I've never had any major trouble with my voice, except on the rare occasions when I've temporarily 'lost my voice' during periods of extreme tiredness. This was Nature's way of saying: 'You've got to let up. I won't let you talk for a few days.'

R.D.   What about the other possible deprivation I mentioned: the delaying or thwarting of an ambition?

D.C.   I've certainly known periods of great difficulty, such as my London College of Divinity days. There was one year (1944–5) when, for the sake of the children, the rest of the family were in Canada while I stayed in London. This entailed the interruption of a marriage relationship which was—and is—infinitely precious.

And there were long periods afterwards when I was at Lingfield, in the heart of Surrey, doing my best to strengthen and enlarge the College while we still couldn't get permission for new premises to be built. Jean and the children were on the other side of London, at Northwood.

This was a time of difficulty for us all—I couldn't call it the thwarting of an ambition—but everyone suffered in some way during or after the war, or both; and many, many people suffered far more than we did.

R.D.   By contrast, what would you say was one of your best periods—perhaps your years in Bradford in the late Fifties?

D.C.   Here again I had a job with a challenge, with opportunities for expansion, creating new pastoral links, and so on. These were my first years as a bishop, and of course there were difficulties, as there are at every stage of life, but on the whole it was certainly a good period.

God has blessed me and watched over me, all through my life. I am so thankful for having had creative work to do, right from the start. Creative work and work with people—given those two, what more can a man ask? Wealth and fame are very secondary matters.

R.D.   What you have just said is especially true today, when technology seems to be reducing the number of really creative jobs.

D.C.   Everyone has a spark of creativity because we are each made in the image of God, the Divine Creator. My heart goes out to people who have to go every day to an uncreative job.

R.D.   In your book *The Heart of the Christian Faith* you quoted Cardinal Suenens—that God is a God of surprises. As you look back on your life, were there any unexpected turning-points?

D.C.   Things seem to have developed fairly naturally: from the headship of the London College of Divinity to a bishopric, to an archbishopric, and then Archbishop of Canterbury. In one sense it is a natural progression—but totally unexpected to me.

If someone had said to me in 1934, 'In 1974 you will be Archbishop of Canterbury', I would have laughed in disbelief. I suppose the unexpected turn came very much earlier: after a rather inhibiting home life, I learned a lot during my public-school days from men such as Padfield and Sargent; then there was the fascination of the work in Hoxton; and a picture forming in my mind, in later schooldays, of a life's work as a parish priest, probably in a run-down area. I couldn't think of anything more fulfilling than that, and in some ways I still cannot.

Then came my university days—the fact that I got a good degree and was beginning to reveal a few God-bestowed gifts in languages and in teaching. This turned the tide from the prospect of being a parish priest to the possibility of combining pastoral and academic work.

R.D. What—or, rather, who—is an Evangelical, and are you one?

D.C. I love that word. It has a good New Testament pedigree: *evangelion* meaning 'the Gospel', 'good news'. I don't mind being called an Evangelical, provided the word is allowed to stand on its own, without another word being hyphenated on to it; and provided it is not given any nuance of exclusiveness.

My roots are in good evangelical soil, and it was a happy coincidence that I went to the College of St. John the Evangelist, Cambridge, of which I am now an Honorary Fellow.

For a short while I was at Wycliffe Hall, Oxford, for theological studies, and there I came under the influence of men such as Douglas Harrison, who was later Archdeacon of Sheffield and Dean of Bristol; Joe Fison, very much like an Old Testament prophet, who became Bishop of Salisbury; and Ralph Taylor, 'Puffy' Taylor as we called him, who became Bishop of Sodor and Man—he radiated a quality of real and deep devotion.

I owe an enormous amount to that trio for their basic honesty, their almost Biblical depth of character, and their intellectual sharpness and probity.

R.D. Last week the producer of a television series, based on world-famous paintings, said: 'We want not only to present paintings and artists; we want to teach people how to observe.' It seems to me that the value of those men was not only the content of what they taught you; they left with you a style, an approach, a reverence for the work.

D.C. Yes, I am sure you are right about the inspiration of a really gifted teacher. It doesn't matter whether or not you can reproduce his comments slavishly; heaven forbid that you should. What is important is that he has introduced you to new books, new minds, new vistas.

R.D. It is almost like acquiring a new pair of eyes, isn't it? You learn to see in a new way. He has, as it were, opened doors for you, and now you can go on and open new doors for yourself.

I wonder how many in a congregation realise the number of people you 'bring' with you—or, rather, who bring you!—as you walk up the steps of the pulpit before a sermon: so many influences, direct ones and subtle ones.

D.C.   Yes, they go on making contributions, like tributaries flowing into the river of one's life and being.

The three men I have mentioned from my time at Wycliffe helped me in the subjects of doctrine and devotion. When I look back on my Cambridge years, 1928–31, I can see that the dons who taught me there influenced me in a different way.

I remember a feeling of awe and of gratitude that I was allowed to sit at the feet of several of the finest scholars in Europe. There was Herbert Loewe, a charming man with an immense knowledge of Rabbinic literature, a practising Jew who had read the Theological Tripos and got a First in it. And S. A. Cook, Regius Professor of Hebrew, whose mind was so full that it overflowed. He had a vast knowledge of the whole Semitic world. His ideas, opinions, and knowledge spilled forth like a tap suddenly opened up: the volume couldn't be held back. Cook's predecessor was R. H. Kennett: you'd go to him for lectures on the Psalms, and he would emend them so radically that by the time you went home for lunch they seemed more the Psalms according to Kennett than the Psalms according to David!

To this day, I have a feeling of privilege for those three years, a member of a small group, seldom more than four or five, learning from men of such quality. I gained the discipline of studying texts in minute detail—Hebrew texts as well as Aramaic, Syriac and Greek—probing for the root meaning of a word and its content, with an exactitude that was very demanding.

Some people might think this was confining, too narrow a syllabus, too narrow a conspectus, but it introduced me to an exact scholarship which I hope has helped save me from imprecision of thought or of expression.

R.D. Has your thorough training in languages helped you in your pastoral work, enabling you to tune in quickly to whoever you were meeting? I am thinking, for example, of your time in Islington, when every day you were meeting people of a background and education very different from your own?

D.C. The change from being a junior don at Manchester University to a curacy in the Islington of the thirties was—to use an over-used word—traumatic. But my teaching period had been extremely valuable: it taught me to express myself clearly.

R.D. And with economy of language?

D.C. Yes, certainly. Having to teach elementary Hebrew to students who could hardly write the characters, I had to keep a sense of priorities and reduce the content to simple stages. I'm sure this was a help to me later on in the pulpit.

But from some points of view I was probably not a very efficient curate. My background was so different from that of, say, a local boy who left school at fourteen and went straight into a factory. I used to feel that the London City Missionary who was attached to our staff was far better suited than I to our work in Islington.

R.D. I wonder if you feel you have learned about the ways of God not only from orthodox sources but also from other people: the agnostic or the non-believer, or people of only brief acquaintance, bringing you a message from God in an unexpected way?

D.C. As the years have gone by, I have become much more ready to learn from people who, in my narrow beginnings, I would never have thought I could learn from. I am shocked, as I look back, to think how quick I was to label people and sometimes mentally dismiss them. One of the joys of my life has been to see how God manifests Himself in so rich a variety of people. The God of many names reveals Himself not only in a Basil Hume or a Cardinal Suenens but also in a Plymouth Brother such as Professor F. F. Bruce or a Quaker such as Gerald Priestland.

Again and again I have felt rebuked—I don't think that is too strong a word—by the lives of people with no Church allegiance who shine with goodness and beauty. The Holy Spirit inspires and nourishes all creation, not just the Body of the Church. And so we ought always to be on the look-out for signs and manifestations of God's activity in spheres beyond what we call the Church.

R.D.   What you have just said reminds me of the evening I went to a school play and sat next to someone who I guessed was a member of the staff. Assuming he was a teacher, I said, 'What do you do here in the school?' And he replied, 'I'm the gardener.' My jaw dropped. I was trapped by my expectations. And for a moment I couldn't relate to him. I didn't have the presence of mind to see what a lucky man he was.

D.C.   When I ask women what they do, some reply, 'Oh, I'm just a mother' or 'I'm just a housewife.' And I say, 'What do you mean, "*just* a mother" or "*just* a housewife"?'

R.D.   While we are talking about people, I wonder if there are any qualities which you observe and admire in others and wish you had more of yourself?

D.C.   The short answer is that there are so many I don't know where to start! In being able to love and be gentle and generous, I feel such a beginner.

R.D.   You have often spoken of the pastoral gifts which your wife has contributed to your joint ministry.

D.C.   Yes, she is much better at dealing with individuals than I am. And why is that? Because she is a woman with a deep wellspring of love and a power of discernment. I long for more *agape*, capacity to love. And for as long as I can remember I have prayed for what St. Paul calls *synesis*, penetration, insight. When I hear a visitor coming up the stairs to see me, I send up an arrow prayer to God that I will get to the heart of what this person wants to talk about. Was the reason he gave in his letter just a means of arranging a meeting? Is there something behind it? What has he really come for?

33

R.D. I was deeply moved when we first met by the way you described your marriage: you said that if you and Jean are apart for even a few hours you still have so much to share when you come together again. I'm sure you can't begin to estimate the value of this precious partnership, to your public as well as your private life.

D.C. How right you are. I derive enormous support by sharing my conversation, my prayer, my whole life, with a good and godly woman. And women are made differently from men, not only physically. We men plod and argue our way towards a solution, whereas women—most annoyingly!—dart through to the answer in a tenth of the time.

R.D. A wise friend once said to me: 'A woman's thinking begins at the point where man's thinking has finished.'

D.C. To have a partner with such quality and speed of perception—on a problem or on another person's character—is a great and continuing strength.

R.D. By contrast, can you call to mind priests in our Communion or in the Roman Catholic Church who are not married and yet whose relationship with God and their fellow-men is strong enough to help them through the ups and downs of life?

D.C. Yes, men such as Trevor Huddleston, and Oliver Allison who spent almost the whole of his ministry in the Sudan. I could think of at least a dozen single men who have brought exceptional love, compassion and creativity to the priesthood.

I think God gives them a kind of extra sense, in almost the same way as a blind person can develop acute hearing, or in the way that Max Warren, one of the great missionary statesmen of this century, lost an eye but continued to read voraciously and found near the end of his life that his one eye was stronger than his wife's two eyes. Nature provides many such examples of compensation.

R.D. Have you been aware in your own family of a mutual influence and complementarity between children and parents?

D.C.   Very much so. We have two daughters, both of them born in Canada and now in their early forties. They have greatly enriched our lives. We are a harmonious quartet and like nothing better than going on holiday together.

They are quite different one from the other. Ann, the older of the two (they are twenty-three months apart), has been a teacher for the whole of her working life. She is a graduate of Edinburgh University and afterwards did a year of teacher-training at Cambridge. She has served in two teaching posts: first at the junior school of St. Lawrence College, Ramsgate, where she worked for about twelve years; and now at the Pilgrims' School, Winchester, where she shows a real gift for teaching boys of seven or eight. She is devoted to them. She also teaches music and plays the flute, and for many years has been closely associated with the National Youth Orchestra. Ann has a great gift for friendship, and adds gaiety and joy to any company of which she is a part.

Our other daughter is Ruth. Ever since she was a child, she wanted to be a doctor, and in her teens she decided to become a missionary doctor, and this is what she is. She took her first degree at Leeds, with its fine medical faculty, and then studied gynaecology at Liverpool. She worked in several hospitals as a house physician and trained as a missionary with the Church Missionary Society, hoping to be sent to Africa.

When she was ready to go abroad, C.M.S. told her that there was an even greater need at that time in Pakistan. This is where she went, and she now has not the slightest doubt that the hand of God guided her to the right place. She feels immensely fulfilled working in a little hospital in a small town called Bannu. She has been there for over eleven years and is prepared to stay until the beckoning hand says, 'Go home' or 'Go elsewhere'.

Ruth is devoted to her patients, most of them illiterate, many of whom arrive by camel or donkey or on foot for such things as their hysterectomy operation or for a baby to be born. This hospital is a godsend in a country where, according to the tenets of Islam, the women cannot be attended to by a male doctor about a gynaecological matter unless they are *in extremis*. It is in Northern Pakistan, only a few miles from the border with Afghanistan, and in the past year or so Ruth has had additional patients from among the refugees.

Ruth, like Ann, feels greatly fulfilled, and she puts all her skills and energy into her work. She is—why shouldn't I say it?—a very good doctor. She is also a good linguist and she speaks both Urdu and Pushtu. Ruth too is musical, though she hasn't much opportunity for that in Bannu.

R.D.   How often do you and your wife manage to see Ann and Ruth?

D.C.   Not nearly as often as we would like, in part because we all lead very active lives and in part because Ruth is only rarely able to visit England.

One of the delightful aspects of having a family is that all of you develop together, and as the children grow up the interchange of mind and spirit becomes increasingly precious: they become friends as well as relatives on a very deep level. Ann and Ruth have brought enormous enrichment to Jean and myself. We are both so thankful to have a happy family with a strong homing instinct.

R.D.   I'm sure you are right when you speak of both generations developing together. I feel it is vital for parents to be able to shed former roles as their children change and mature and find their individuality.

D.C.   Yes, and not try to clip their wings. You have to let them go at the right time. Jesus spoke of this same need for creative separation from one's parents (Matt. 19:5).

All four of us share an interest in music and literature, and, at the deepest level, we share a commitment to Christ.

The tragedy of many homes is that the parents don't find enough time to be with their children. Misunderstandings increase and this leads to all kinds of trouble later on.

R.D.   While we are on the subject of people, perhaps you would like to tell of some of the most memorable people you have met. Lewis and Eliot were colleagues on the Commission for the revision of the Psalter. And you knew Fisher, didn't you?

D.C.   T. S. Eliot I knew only slightly, a tall, bent figure, suffering that dreadful disease of the lungs, emphysema. It was a privilege to work with him.

And, as you say, C. S, Lewis was there also, a chain-smoker, looking like an old countryman with a ruddy complexion. Slung over his shoulder was his haversack, stuffed with books and papers.

These two men, with their wealth of knowledge of English literature, converged from their different standpoints to help the Commission. We did our best to put the translation provided by the Hebraists into language which wouldn't differ too radically from the style of Coverdale and yet could be sung to Anglican chants.

My contact with Lewis and Eliot was largely due to Geoffrey Fisher. He had a delightful way of emerging from his study at Lambeth with his glasses high on his forehead. Then, shifting them down on to the bridge of his nose, he would say 'Oh, Coggan, I want you to be in charge of . . .' Thanks to him, I was Chairman of the Liturgical Commission for four years (1960–4). I also chaired two other Commissions, working on the revision of the Psalter and of the Catechism.

Fisher was a remarkable man. People constantly refer to him as the 'schoolmaster-Archbishop'—he had been Headmaster of Repton for many years—but he was much more than an able administrator. He could be stern on matters of discipline and make you feel like a schoolboy trembling on the headmaster's mat, but Fisher was a man of love and caring in his pastoral work, as I saw at first-hand with several personal crises he handled.

He did not try to be a second William Temple, a philosopher-theologian, but in his own way Fisher was God's gift to the Church at a time when finances and buildings needed special attention after the Second World War. God endows His Church with people of different gifts: some are apostles, some prophets, some administrators, some evangelists.

R.D Was Temple an influence you drew upon?

D.C. Only through his writings. When I came back to England from Canada in 1944 to take up my appointment with the London College of Divinity, I longed to meet Temple and get to know him, but he died only a few months later.

R.D. What was there about his writings which inspired you?

D.C Among other things, what he achieved, for example, in *Readings in St. John's Gospel*: the ability to use his massive mind and learning in the service of exegesis.

R.D. My father, who was at Rugby a few years after Temple, told me a little story about him which you may not know. I gather he was rather short and fat, and because of this there was a short training run nicknamed 'Billy's Belch'.

D.C. I like the way he spoke of his difficulties with arithmetic while working on his personal accounts. 'I tot them up from the top to the bottom and get one result. I then tot them up from the bottom to the top and get another result. Then I add them together and divide by two!'

3   HIGH OFFICE

R.D.   I feel we should start with the earlier years.

D.C.   Yes, as I look back I can see that God has been very gracious in preparing me for the challenges and opportunities which have come in the latter part of my ministry.

For example, I had those twelve years, strenuous years, as Principal of the London College of Divinity. I am immensely thankful for the experience I gained in administration. In those wartime and post-war years, I had only a small staff, no bursar and not much secretarial help, and so I had to do a lot of the day-to-day admin work. Often I longed to be freer for the scholarly side of my post, and for more personal contact with individuals, but I can now see what a useful preparation this was for my time as a Bishop and Archbishop, however much one may delegate to others. Perhaps this is an illustration of St. Paul's dictum that 'in everything God works together for good with those who love him' (Rom. 8:28, RSV).

R.D.   Were you ever given an intimation that one day you would become Archbishop of Canterbury?

D.C.   It had certainly never occurred to me until I was coming to the end of my time in Canada.

H. J. Cody used to fill St. Paul's, Toronto, with a large and fashionable congregation and, like a prophet himself, expound the prophets to them at great length. He then became President of the University of Toronto. When I went to tell him that I was going to leave to be Principal of the London College of Divinity, he said to me, semi-seriously, 'Coggan, one day you'll be Archbishop of Canterbury.' That meeting, more than thirty-five years before any appointment, was the nearest I ever got to thinking about Canterbury.

R.D.   How did you first hear that you were being considered as the next Primate of All England?

D.C. When it became known that Michael Ramsey was going to retire, people started guessing, as they always do, who would succeed him. My name was mentioned, I suppose, among the leading half-dozen. Then the Prime Minister, Harold Wilson, asked me to go and see him. He asked me straight out and said he wanted to submit my name to the Queen.

R.D. Please take us back to that day. How did you react, inwardly and outwardly?

D.C. He probably would have liked me to have given an answer then and there, but I didn't feel I could, so I told him I needed time to discuss it with my wife and pray about it.

R.D. How long did you feel you wanted?

D.C. Not a long time, perhaps three or four days. My wife and I have always been extremely close in the work and life we have shared together, and I felt it would have been entirely wrong to go back to Cambridge, where we were staying at the time, and say, 'My dear, we're going to Canterbury.'

It would be a big step for her as well as for me to leave York, where we had spent thirteen happy years, and go to Canterbury for what we knew would probably be only five or six years (though there was no regulation decreeing that I had to retire when I did).

We, who loved the north of England, would have to move to two large residences, one in Lambeth and the other in Canterbury, and adopt a new manner of life.

R.D. And how did Jean respond?

D.C. She has always been marvellous at times of change. She simply said that if I felt it was right to accept, then she would of course give me her total support. So we undertook the new work together.

R.D. I'd be glad if we could look back briefly to the time when Michael Ramsey was appointed to Canterbury, and York became vacant. Harold Macmillan was Prime Minister.

D.C. That was in 1961. We met at the Admiralty because

No. 10 was being redecorated. He said that Geoffrey Fisher was about to announce his retirement, but I left Mr. Macmillan at the end of our hour together not sure what he had in mind for me. What he must have been pondering, I suppose, was which of the senior Sees to recommend me for: Canterbury, York or London.

As I look back, I am profoundly thankful for the way things worked out. I went to Canterbury at the age of sixty-five, which some might say was rather late, but I went there with the experience of nineteen years in the episcopate, a marvellous training. First I had five and a half happy years as Bishop of Bradford, a relatively small diocese and a beautiful one, extending right up the Yorkshire moors. There I learned how to be a bishop, or tried to. Then came thirteen and a half years in the great See of York, a far larger diocese, with three suffragan bishops, three archdeacons, and oversight of the Northern Province—Primate of England but not Primate of All England. I regard those nineteen years as a gracious provision by God in training and equipping me for the work at Canterbury.

Conversation at my meeting with Macmillan ranged widely: here was a man with enormous experience of life and people, now a patrician figure. I remember his telling me about his friendship with Ronnie Knox who tried in vain to persuade him to leave the Church of England for the Roman Catholic Church. Macmillan also told me of the day when Ronnie came to No. 10 looking very ill. Macmillan sent him to see Lord Evans. Ronnie returned from the consultation with a sentence of death. There could be no hope of recovery: he had cancer. When they were parting Ronnie said, 'I'm going on a very long journey.' They never met again.

R.D.   You said a moment ago that it was comparatively late for you to go to Canterbury in your mid-sixties, and yet you recently spoke to me of the sixties as being a suitable decade for undertaking high office because of a combination of experience of life and, with God's grace, some years of good health and reserves of energy still to come. What then are your reflections about the timing?

D.C. My only regret is that little more than five years is rather short for a great office. You come to the end of the period and ask yourself, 'How much have I left undone?' I am not saying I wanted to go to Canterbury earlier—I was happy and fulfilled at York—but there are risks, of health for example, in a man of sixty-five going to a job as demanding as Canterbury. You have to go absolutely full-tilt; and at any moment an emergency may crop up, in any part of the world, needing to be dealt with right away. The demands made are constant. But given good health, as thank God I was, I was able to avoid the major risks.

R.D. Now please take us back to the time of your enthronement.

D.C. I became Archbishop of Canterbury in December 1974: the legal processes were completed in the crypt of St. Paul's Cathedral. The enthronement took place on January 24th, the eve of St. Paul's Day, 1975. On the next day I was given a magnificent service of welcome at Westminster Abbey.

R.D. Were there any particular goals, or framework, or direction, that you set yourself, even if you may not have wanted to say so publicly at the time?

D.C. Before going to Canterbury I had a chance to think and plan and pray, but leaving York entailed a lot of work and we had many goodbyes to say.

I longed for the Church of England to become more outward-looking, less concerned with its own committee machinery and more concerned for the thousands of unchurched people in England, and more outward-reaching to the world beyond our shores. The danger for people living on an island is insularity.

I hope it is true to say that more attention is now given to evangelistic outreach than there was a decade ago—take, for example, the Nationwide Initiative in Evangelism. I can only pray that this is so.

At the same time I looked towards the Anglican Communion world-wide. I was fortunate to have travelled quite widely in my York days, and during my time at Canterbury I undertook some long and strenuous journeys, not only ecclesiastical journeys to church leaders, but also, for example for visits to the Forces, in Germany and elsewhere.

R.D. The media often speak of a current crisis of identity for the Church and the priesthood. Some commentators speak of this subject relentlessly, almost to the point of cliché, but there may well be an underlying truth. For example, other professions—social work, counselling, some aspects of teaching—have made incursions into the traditional work of the priesthood, leaving many Churches and their ministers unsure of their role. Was this something you tried to examine anew?

D.C. Yes, constantly. I think of my wife's maternal grandfather, who for forty-two years was rector of a small parish in Norfolk. He and his daughters were the hub of all good works, visiting and caring for the poor and distressed—a social service in themselves!

The State has taken over much of the welfare and educational work previously done by the Church. Many priests are now saying, 'What is left for us?' and this led me to do all I could to help the clergy at a personal level. I found myself thinking privately and often saying publicly that, although a bishop has to be a leader, he is also what I call 'a backroom boy', there to support the men and women who are in the front line. And so I seized every possible opportunity to join clergy and lay people on Retreats or Quiet Days. I often spoke about the function of the Church in today's society. I encouraged all members of the Church to help the parish priest and allow him the time, the scope and the freedom to fulfil his own special contribution.

To be a man of prayer and of spiritual study; to preach from the pulpit; to be a man of the sacraments—no State can take over these functions. These are the essentials of Christian ministry, and the clergy need to be under-girded by their bishops and archbishops. I wanted my clergy, in the midst of a rapidly-changing society, to be able to work thankfully and with humble pride. I can best sum up the task I set myself as 'a ministry of encouragement'.

R.D. During your term of office you travelled widely. What do you see as the main issues facing the world, the Church and the individual?

D.C. First of all there is the great divide between rich and poor: twenty per cent of the world's population possessing eighty per cent of the world's food and energy resources; the disparity which Barbara Ward, for example, tried with such passion to warn us of; the inequality which can light the flame of war.

Next, there is racial intolerance. In recent riots in this country, these two issues, race and poverty, seem to have coalesced, triggered also by poor housing, unemployment and lack of purpose in life.

On the religious front, we are witnessing the rising power of Islam combined with enormous wealth brought about by the sale of oil. You have only to travel to West Africa, as I did in March 1979, to see how the influence of Islam is spreading down from the north.

In the heart of London and other big cities in England we now have Muslim temples. Are we taking an intelligent look at Islam? And are we looking deeply enough? Are we equipping ourselves for an interplay of minds?

The haves and have-nots; the tensions within a multi-racial society; the advance of Islam; the relationship between Communist and non-Communist countries; and the increasing mobility of families—all these constitute problems as well as challenges for the Church.

R.D. You spoke of inequality as one of the causes of war. Mutual fear and distrust, and the armaments race which is their terrifying outcome—here is another possible cause of war.

D.C. It is a kind of international madness that so much money is being spent on arms, rather than more money going towards basic necessities of food, clothing, housing, education and literacy. Succeeding generations will look back with astonishment that men could indulge in such folly.

The Brandt Report (*North-South: A Programme for Survival*) notes the 'terrible irony that the most dynamic and rapid transfer of highly sophisticated equipment and technology from rich to poor countries has been in the machinery of death'.

The Report estimates that the world's annual military bill (in 1979) is 450 billion US dollars, while official development aid accounts for less than five per cent of that figure. The Report gives several cost comparisons:

—the price of one jet fighter could fund 40,000 village pharmacies;
—a modern tank costs about one million dollars: that sum of money could provide 1,000 classrooms to help educate 30,000 children;
—one half of one per cent of one year's world military expenditure would pay for all the farm equipment needed to increase food production and approach self-sufficiency in food–deficit low-income countries by 1990.

R.D. This is one of the paradoxes of our time: the expansion of armaments and the increasing nuclear threat coincide with our growing understanding of human psychology, our concern for the environment, our exploration of the planets, our awareness of the inter-relatedness of all people and nations.

D.C. Only the spread of the gospel of love, as expounded in the Christian faith, can redeem the plight and danger we all face.

R.D. Going back to your time at Canterbury: what were the high points, the initiatives in which your hopes were fulfilled?

D.C. One of the high points was certainly the Lambeth Conference of 1978. I faced the Conference with an element of awe and trembling. Here were four hundred and fifty bishops from all over the world, coming together for three weeks. To be chairman of such a gathering is an immense responsibility, and things could so easily have gone wrong. There were issues—such as the ordination of women—which could have

45

strained the Communion almost to breaking-point. At the end of the Conference I felt thankful for God's mercy in holding us together.

The first Lambeth Conference was in 1867. They are held every ten years or so, always in England, and have been formative in the evolution of the Anglican Communion. Our 1978 Conference was the first to be residential, and this made a major contribution to the value and depth of our discussions. We allowed ample time for prayer and worship—including a daily Eucharist—as well as time for getting to know each other, between sessions and often far into the night.

I had attended the 1958 and 1968 Conferences, and at the latter I had presided over one of the three main divisions: the one that dealt with Ministry. I knew some of the problems and wanted to put them right. On looking back, I felt there were many disadvantages in meeting on a daily non-residential basis. It was hard enough for those of us who were conditioned to buses and tube-trains at rush-hours, morning and evening. It was much more wearing for bishops who did not know their way around London. And a Conference organised on a daily basis gave us too little time to pray together and come to know one another in depth.

Had the Conference been in London, it would have been difficult for individual delegates to turn down the large number of social invitations from families and friends, and so we thought it would be a marvellous idea to go to Canterbury, the rock whence we were hewn! The University is only a couple of miles from the centre of Canterbury, so residential accommodation and meeting halls could easily be provided. The university staff, at all levels, did everything possible to make us happy and comfortable; and we could look out, from our conference room, on the Cathedral in all its historic beauty.

We soon came to know one another, and with a new degree of intimacy. This, in itself, was one of the great benefits of the Conference. We learned the particular problems which each bishop was contending with in his part of the world, be it Africa or Latin America or the Far East. In future we were able to picture each other as human beings, not just names on a prayer list.

Every day we were able to worship together unhurriedly, and every day the Eucharist was celebrated according to one of the rites of a country within the Anglican Communion, in which we could all share.

We also had a number of social activities. I especially remember the evening at the Cathedral when the University conferred honorary degrees on Archbishop Simms of Armagh, Bishop Coburn of Massachusetts, and Bishop Tutu, General Secretary of the South African Council of Churches. The ceremony was conducted with dignity as well as some touches of humour.

One day we went by coach and by car to London, and the weather favoured us. After lunch, which was served in the Lambeth Palace garden, we crossed the river and filled Westminster Abbey for a magnificent service at which all the bishops were in their Convocation robes. Then we went to Buckingham Palace for a garden party where the Queen Mother made us welcome; the Queen was in Canada for the opening of the Commonwealth Games. At the end of a memorable day we went back home to Canterbury.

The wives of the bishops had a mini-Lambeth of their own, lasting eight days, also in Canterbury, where Jean and a team of helpers arranged a varied programme. At some of the main Conference events, such as the degree night and the visit to London, we were joined by the wives who, each in her own way, share deeply in the work of the Church.

The Conference Report listed thirty-seven resolutions, covering a very wide range of topics, because a decade would elapse before we met again. Many of the subjects would continue to be live issues for many years to come. I shall summarise as best I can under four headings.

First, the relationship between the affluent, technologically-advanced nations and the relatively poor nations in Asia, Africa and Latin America; and the need for us to see ourselves not only as givers but also as potential recipients.

Second, the question of the centre of authority in the

Anglican Communion—where is it to be found? This subject was raised again and again, and I felt constrained to speak on it towards the end of the Conference.

Third, and importantly, ethics in a rapidly changing world, yielding a whole nest of new and profound problems: sexual ethics, medical ethics, human rights, marriage and the increasing divorce rate.

Fourth, problems specific to our own work-roles and responsibilities. What does it mean to belong to the Church of Christ in a world in agony? Can our Anglican Communion hold together and reconcile its internal differences in a spirit of love and trust? Differences, for example, over the ordination of women, and between the liberal and conservative approaches to liturgy and the Bible.

This, I trust, is sufficient to illustrate how widely we discussed and how profitably we met.

R.D.   What were some of the other highlights of your years at Canterbury?

D.C.   So many things happened and it is hard for me to select. I passed rapidly from one activity to another, moved on by the impetus of events. I shall always remember the service in St. Paul's which made so fitting a climax to the Queen's jubilee year (1977). And there were tragic occasions such as the State Funeral in Westminster Abbey for Lord Mountbatten; the Memorial Service in St. Paul's at which the Prince of Wales gave the address; and in Mersham, Kent, the funeral of two other members of the family who were killed at the same time, the Dowager Lady Brabourne and her thirteen-year-old grandson, one of twins.

I undertook some long journeys abroad, each something of a drama of its own, ranging from a short European trip to a long trek around the dioceses of West Africa in March 1979.

Three years earlier, Jean and I went to the Sudan. Just before we left home we were told that a killer plague had broken out in the south, not far from Juba where I was to inaugurate a Province. In Khartoum the President arranged a party for us in his palace gardens by the Nile. As we parted, he assured us that it would be safe for us to make the trip, and he lent us his private plane. We travelled a thousand miles down the Nile to Juba and were greeted—if I may pun—by a jubilant crowd: we were the first visitors to have been allowed in for some time. The inauguration took place in a packed Cathedral on a roastingly hot day, and then the Vice-President of the Sudan, a fine Christian, provided a celebration feast. That same evening we flew back to Khartoum. This was a truly memorable occasion in the history of the growth of the Christian Church.

Bishop Gwynne (1863–1957), whose portrait you can see over there, was a dear friend of mine and a graduate of the London College of Divinity, of which, long after his time there, I was to become Principal. Around the turn of the century he was a pioneer missionary in the Sudan. Thanks to his early work, the Church there has rooted firmly and been strong enough to withstand severe persecution. By a happy coincidence, I was the person who was to inaugurate the Province in which all four Bishops, including the man I made Archbishop, are black. Indeed the majority of the clergy in the Sudan are black.

R.D.   Do you look back on any disappointments?

D.C.   Yes, there were two major disappointments: first, the breakdown of the Anglican–Methodist negotiations on unity. I presided at the meeting of the General Synod when the voting took place. As Chairman, I tried very hard to look non-committal. Everybody knew what my own views were, and they told me I did not succeed very well in hiding the disappointment which showed on my face. That was one of the saddest days of my life. Another disappointment was the negative vote on the ordination of women, a subject you will no doubt want to talk about later.

R.D.   Are there any opportunities which, with hindsight, you could have grasped more firmly; or decisions taken which you now question?

D.C.   When you look back, you can always see the imperfections of your work. Twenty years on, others will be able to give a better answer to your question than the man who only emerged a few months ago from the heat of the battle.

There were some very controversial issues such as the re-marriage in church of divorced people. At a meeting of the General Synod, the Bishop of Lichfield's Report was debated, and I had a share in defeating one or two of the Report's main motions, which—while always being open to change—I felt might lead to laxity in the Church's standards for marriage and divorce.

One can only hope and pray that better ways forward will be found, such as the current experiment in Canada where in certain dioceses the Bishop appoints a small group of highly-qualified people to make recommendations to him. He is then empowered to make a decision about the remarriage of divorced persons in Church.

These are borderline issues, complex and finely-balanced, involving deeply personal feelings. Fair and just solutions will evolve in their own time.

R.D. How did you manage to keep your sense of priorities among the many different roles you had to fulfil?

D.C. I always made ample time for department heads who wanted to come and see me, such as the Secretary of the Crown Appointments Commission, or Bishop John Howe from the Anglican Consultative Council, or the Secretary-General of the General Synod, or the Secretary of the Counsellors on Foreign Relations. I gave high priority to top level interchange of minds.

My chaplains, both Senior and Domestic, knew that I was always ready to see at short notice anybody in distress or crisis or deep need: this could range from a marital problem to a local difficulty which for some reason had not been resolved at Suffragan level.

I tried never to neglect preparation for what I was called on to say from pulpit, public platform, radio or television. It is an insult to an audience to speak unprepared, just as it would be an insult for a musician not to have done his practice.

R.D. Did you manage, then, to keep a reasonable balance between scheduled and unscheduled time?

D.C. I hope so. I was always prepared for a day's plans to be altered because of some emergency. Afterwards you have to face a backlog of work piled high on your desk.

R.D. You must have worked long hours, and yet I know how blessed you were to have Jean's support throughout your working weeks, both at Lambeth and at Canterbury.

D.C. I travelled from Lambeth to Canterbury late on Fridays, and always with a heavy bag of work. There I had only one chaplain, the telephone wasn't such a tyranny, and the number of visitors was less.

Weekends, apart from engagements in and near Canterbury, gave me an opportunity to catch up on any backlog of work and prepare for the meetings and speeches of the coming week. I'd return to London on the Sunday night or the Monday morning having done a weekend's work but feeling renewed by the change of surroundings and the peace of Canterbury.

R.D. A few minutes ago you spoke about the impetus of events. How did you manage the shift of attention from, say, a pastoral matter to a committee meeting and then to a public engagement, all within a short space of time, each calling on a different side of your personality?

D.C. The variety helped to keep me fresh: I would go from a personal interview to a meeting of the Church Commissioners or to preside over the Standing Committee of the General Synod where a different approach is needed.

You have a man sitting in a chair opposite you, and your whole attention is concentrated on him: you are wondering what question to ask him so that he can clarify his dilemma. Then you go into a room full of men and women, each with a keen intellect, and as Chairman you wonder not only how to quieten, without being rude, the person who talks too much, but also how to elicit comments from the quieter members, how to bring out from these able people the best they can give, and then at the end shape their contributions into a series of resolutions.

51

Committee work is a fascinating art. As Chairman you have to keep a balance, not wasting time and yet not hurrying people unduly. And you aim to finish before everyone gets tired and bad-tempered. If the committee can see you are playing your part, and enabling them to play theirs, they will do their best for you, rather like the co-operation between an orchestra and its conductor.

R.D. I'd be interested to hear what else you feel you have learned about the art of chairmanship. I share with Colin Morris a fear of 'death by a thousand committees'!

D.C. That reminds me of a saying, 'The ideal committee is a committee of two, one of whom is ill.' I don't believe that. And the fact that I don't believe it is linked with the doctrine of the Holy Spirit.

Our Lord knew how to make the best use of a team and weld its individual members together. He drew into His circle a wide variety of people, different in age, in occupation, in personality and temperament, and in religious and political affiliation.

There was Peter, gifted with powers of insight but sometimes rash in speech; a born leader, and yet he would quail at the sneer of a servant girl. By contrast we have John, a younger man, perhaps in his late teens or early twenties, mystical, meditative, as quiet as Peter was ebullient.

Then consider Matthew, a Jewish tax-gatherer, despised by his fellow Jews because he earned his living from the hated Romans. At the opposite political extreme was Simon the Zealot, who we imagine might have carried a dagger under his cloak, poised ready for any Jew who betrayed his cause to the Romans. And yet they were all brothers, unified by their love of Jesus and by His love for them.

Among the women who were followers of Jesus was Joanna, wife of Chuza, Herod's steward; and, by contrast, Mary Magdalene whom tradition has described as a woman of the streets (Luke 8:2). Thus were social barriers overcome.

In Galatians (3:28) St. Paul expressed this unity so beautifully: 'There is neither Jew nor Greek, there is neither bond nor free, there is neither male nor female: for ye are all one in Christ Jesus.'

The followers of Jesus were like human spokes of a divine wheel: the nearer they came to the hub, the holy centre, the Christ, the nearer they came to one another, transcending all man-made barriers and surface differences. Here we have a model for the Church—in all places and in every epoch.

I've seen the Holy Spirit inspire a heterogeneous group, enabling it to arrive at a united approach and make worthwhile decisions. A committee can be creative. That is why I enjoy and value it.

R.D. During your years at Canterbury, did you and your wife allow yourselves real holidays, free even of preaching appointments?

D.C. I used to urge clergy to take one day off each week but I found I could rarely get round to this myself. The most I found time for was a short refresher: a walk in the country or a few hours in the garden.

We always tried to keep August free. I would often come back home halfway through a holiday and spend a couple of days reducing the pile of letters and dealing with any urgent matters. I always took a bag of books and papers away with me and used August as a month for reading as well as preparation for special events I was due to attend in the autumn. But above all August was a time to refresh mind and body.

In addition to my main holiday, we used to go away once or twice a year for a few days. My secretary wouldn't phone or send on letters unless there was something urgent. As in August, I would take some work with me, but at least we could lie-in in the mornings: for a few days we didn't have to get up at half-past six.

At Lambeth we literally lived above the shop: our flat was on a floor above the offices—mine and those of my chaplains and secretaries. To get away from the building itself made a welcome change, much as we loved the people we worked with.

R.D. To what extent were you able to keep in touch with the everday pastoral needs of clergy and parishioners?

D.C. Suffragan Bishops and Archdeacons did most of the day-to-day work of my diocese, but at weekends I often travelled in order to do my share of preaching, confirming, celebrating Holy Communion and instituting Vicars to their parishes. This was a great joy.

Once a month we had a staff meeting at which the Area Bishops, the three Archdeacons, my Domestic Chaplain and I would come together for a celebration of Holy Communion, a working morning, and then lunch. This taking counsel together helped to unite the work of the Diocese and helped me to keep in touch with what was going on.

Then there is the Croydon area of Canterbury Diocese which is the Primate's responsibility in conjunction with the Suffragan Bishop of that area. From my base in London I would often go there on a weekday evening for a confirmation service or an institution.

Clergy and lay people came to see me at Lambeth during the week and at Canterbury during weekends. I also kept in touch by writing a pastoral letter in the monthly diocesan paper.

Sometimes I would go away for a residential weekend with my Archbishop's Council or the Diocesan Synod, enabling me to explore issues in greater depth. And I shall always remember the day when we invited clergy and retired clergy and many lay workers and their wives to come to Canterbury Cathedral for worship and discussion.

These were some of the many ways in which I tried to show the Church that its father-in-God did deeply care about his family, even though he often had to be an absentee father.

R.D. Perhaps you would like to say something about your travels and what you and the Church learned from them.

D.C. I felt strongly that we British, an island people, sometimes become insular and our vision becomes too narrow: we tend to forget that we are part of a great Anglican Communion and, beyond our own Church, part of a great Church-militant all over the world.

Soon after I went to Canterbury I invited a most gifted man, the Reverend A. C. Oommen, to come and live for a year in our diocese. He is an Indian who has served in Africa. This is a rare combination. We didn't want him to address huge meetings—this isn't his forte. We asked him to travel freely throughout the diocese, meeting small groups and sharing his insights and his love of Christ. He was a benediction to us, and I want our Church to encourage many more similar visits.

'Mutual responsibility and interdependence in the Body of Christ'—a concept which arose from the 1963 Anglican Congress in Toronto—means not only the West giving to the younger Churches but also the younger Churches giving to the West: the depth of an Indian's perception of life and man; the joy and hope of young African Christians; their radical questioning of our methods, our structure, our committee work, forcing us to ask new questions about ourselves. For example, we have such a lot to learn from the Church in East Africa which in recent decades has had a liberating experience by being open to the Holy Spirit.

R.D. And the Church in North America . . .?

D.C. Yes, they have much to teach us. They have generosity and resilience, and the ability to organise the work of a parish on a business-like basis.

My experience of the Church had been wholly English, through boyhood, university life in Cambridge and Manchester, and my curacy in Islington, until we went to live in North America. There, in Canada, a vast country, young and prosperous, I saw Anglicanism in a different and larger setting. Canada, and my visits across the border to the United States, offered, as it were, an open window on the Anglican Communion of which I was to see so much in later years.

R.D. What impressions did you bring back from your visit to Russia in 1977?

D.C. I went to Moscow and Kiev, and also to Zagorsk, just to the north of Moscow, where there is a large seminary for Orthodox priests.

I found it deeply moving to go to Orthodox services in Russia, the churches full of both young and old. Many of the women were widowed during the last war: despite their age they still worship, mostly standing for up to three hours. Their devotion and their haunting music, beautifully sung, give a dramatic edge to their services.

I went also to a Baptist church and to a couple of synagogues, knowing what a difficult time many of the Jews have had. The Jews I worshipped with were mostly elderly. A few synagogues are open and flourishing, but on the whole the Jews are under pressure: there is a shortage of rabbis and not enough centres or facilities for the teaching of Hebrew, Jewish culture and religious knowledge to young people.

I returned so *thankful* for the freedom which most of us take for granted.

R.D.   Then in 1979 you went to Berlin, East Germany and Hungary.

D.C.   The leaders there profess their countries' religious liberty but, whatever may be written in the constitution, you know who is likely to get a job or a university place if two people, one a Marxist and one a Christian, are candidates.

East Germany looked far more prosperous than it did fifteen years earlier when it seemed grey and drab, and many shops were short of basic goods. But Christians still suffer year after year in many subtle ways.

R.D.   I'd be glad at this stage if you would comment on relationships with Rome.

D.C.   In April 1977, just over a year before he died, I had a long audience with Pope Paul VI. We talked openly about the obstacles to reconciliation, such as the marriage of Catholics and non-Catholics. He was then old and easily tired but exceptionally courteous and loving.

Archbishop Geoffrey Fisher—whose widow recently cele-brated her ninetieth birthday—made the breakthrough in December 1960, just before he retired: he was the first Archbishop of Canterbury since the Reformation to visit Rome and have an audience with the Pope (John XXIII). Fisher's initiative was followed up by Archbishop Michael Ramsey, and then by myself; and now, while we talk together, Archbishop Runcie is in Africa meeting Pope John Paul II.

I went again to Rome for the enthronement of John Paul II. I was the first Archbishop of Canterbury since the Reformation to attend a Pope's enthronement: this was another step forward in the relationship between our two Churches. Young people look at me with disbelief when I remind them that not so many years ago a Roman Catholic was not allowed to say the Lord's Prayer in public with a non-Catholic.

We now do so much together: in prayer and worship; in discussion of moral questions; in ecumenical co-operation for social action and reforms. This movement must continue on two levels.

First, the level of theological debate and discussion. Some of the best intellects of both Churches are exchanging thoughts, reaching beyond the controversies of the Reformation back to the New Testament and the days of the early Fathers. By doing this, they are seeing inter-Church relationships with less distortion than if they began with Luther and Cranmer and concentrated on the controversies of recent centuries. The emergence of the three Agreed Statements marks a real step forward and is a good example of the creative work that is being done. The three Statements, signed by the Anglican and Roman Catholic International Commission, are on Eucharistic Doctrine (1971), Ministry and Ordination (1973) and Authority in the Church (1976).

Second, relations can deepen at parish level. The Vicar gets to know the Roman Catholic priest. Lay people from local churches learn how each other worships; they learn about the doctrine of the other Church; where possible, they combine to give expression to Christian insights and witness.

All along, I have pressed for movement towards inter-communion. One of the main obstacles is the difficulty the Catholic Church has in accepting the validity of our Orders: the validity of Anglican ordination to the priesthood and the episcopate. But there are many Catholics who long to see a way round the problem. If we can resolve these basic issues, I am certain that, by receiving Communion together, we shall be given new strength for ecumenical co-operation.

R.D.   You preached a brave sermon in Rome in April 1977.

D.C.   Some would say it was rash! In the heart of Rome I raised this vital question of intercommunion between Anglicans and Roman Catholics. I took a similar stance when I preached in Westminster Cathedral in January 1978. Out of courtesy, and because I was on his territory, I agreed my text with Cardinal Basil Hume. We are close friends and colleagues in Christ.

R.D.   This brings us to the subject of public relations, not only between one Church and another but between you—when you were at Canterbury—and the press, radio and television.

D.C.   There were times, I admit, when I wished the media didn't exist. I might be coming back from a long tour abroad, feeling a bit jaded from jet-lag, and wanting only one thing—a good night's sleep. This is not the ideal moment to be met by an array of cameras and pressmen.

On the other hand, these men and women have to earn a living, they have been commissioned to get a story and some pictures, and they can be a useful aid to the work of the Church if they convey, without distortion, what is on one's mind after a trip aboard or a major world event.

The Church of England has a department at Westminster, led by John Miles, which eases the publicity path for an archbishop. John Miles travelled with me on many of my journeys and had often scheduled in advance my meetings with press, radio and television. He also sent back to England reports of my travels and of statements I made. On the whole I feel I had a good relationship with the media.

R.D.   We have been talking about some of the larger issues, some of the historic events, and I think that many people imagine the life of an Archbishop of Canterbury to be rather intense and serious. But during those years there must have been many small-scale human moments, and also some amusing ones.

D.C.   There was a lot of laughter during my five years at Lambeth. A good many guffaws emanated from my room. I cannot imagine life without humour, especially when things are busy, tense and demanding.

I sometimes experience a memorable moment when I least expect it. I'll give you an illustration. One Sunday morning in mid-winter, shortly before I retired, Jean and I visited a little church. The building was insignificant, its setting not especially pretty, and the music hardly comparable with what we were used to hearing in Canterbury Cathedral! But something deeply moving happened at that Eucharist: it was congregational, everybody playing a part. I felt Heaven draw near.

After the service we had coffee in the church. As I moved among the people and spoke with them, I said to myself, 'This is a house of God, a gate of Heaven, and He is here.' I sensed that, through the ministry of the priest and his colleagues, God was reaching out with love to His people.

R.D.   It is said that with age most people tend to become more cautious. What do you feel is the ideal age, or decade of one's life, to assume high office? I'm thinking not only of the Church but of leadership in any field of life. Energy, vision, maturity, flexibility, the art of delegation—there are so many demands.

D.C.   I don't believe one can be dogmatic about this because each person is an individual with his own make-up and personality, his own background, his own ambitions and destiny.

When I look back on my Cambridge days, I learned more from S. A. Cook than from anyone else. He was a man in his late fifties or early sixties who became Professor of Hebrew for only a short time because of the age limit. His mind was ripe and clear, his knowledge immense and outflowing. What a loss it would have been to Hebrew scholarship if he had been forced to retire a few years earlier.

Some people are old and worn-out at sixty-five; others can

go on working for some years more without signs of strain. Geoffrey Fisher, who retired at seventy-five, said to me that he knew it was time to retire when he began to dread the arrival of his morning mail instead of greeting it with *élan*.

I deprecate any forcing of people into retirement too early: this robs the community of ripeness of judgment and accumulated wisdom.

R.D. When writing a few years ago about the monarchy, John Grigg said that when an institution is under pressure it tends to over-react in one of two ways: by trying to join the trendy throng or by retreating into isolation. Were you aware of trying to keep the balance between change, creativity and free expression, and the need for continuity, for the preservation of eternal truths?

D.C. Are you thinking, for example, of the drive for revision of services, and of the so-called 'social gospel', and of the Church's desire to be seen to be relevant to the twentieth century?

R.D. Yes.

D.C. I have always been pro-revision and I believe that most of the recent liturgical changes have enlivened parish worship. Liturgy and language must be given the freedom to *live* and *move*. I should be very sorry to see the 1662 Prayer Book forgotten and not used, but I also welcome new versions.

To go for the new, just because it is new, is folly. When I look at a friend's bookshelf, I look for some of the classics as well as for more recent writing. For me the best English book on preaching in this century was, and still is, P. T. Forsyth's *Positive Preaching and the Modern Mind*. It was published in 1907 and still hasn't been superseded. Lightfoot on St. Paul, and George Adam Smith on Isaiah and the other Prophets: these commentaries were written a long time ago but they contain many treasures. They must continue to stand alongside the modern books which week by week flow out from the presses.

You mentioned the social gospel: it is immensely important. When you read the Prophets, you see they were men with a social gospel. When you read Deuteronomy, you see intimate love and care for the stranger, for the poor, and even for cattle.

Religion without a strong social commitment is worthless, but social commitment is not the whole gospel: it is a facet, an outgrowth, of the basic teachings. Much harm is done by people who over-emphasise the social gospel and minimise the roots from which it comes: the great doctrinal truths of God and man, judgment, redemption and resurrection.

So, you see, I am a 'both/and' man. But all our theology is 'both/and' theology: human and divine, corporate and individual, joy and suffering, sacrifice and victory, love in prayer and love in action. Here we have a series of paradoxes, too vast for human comprehension, but woe betide you if you choose one and neglect the other. This is rather like a violin string: keep it taut at both ends and you can make music; if one end breaks loose—twang!

R.D. Another thing often said of leaders—in whatever field—is that they are often changed by being in high office: some grow, almost visibly, and meet new responsibilities; others become more cautious, more tentative. Were you changed by those last years when you were so much in the public eye?

D.C. I'm not sure I can answer that; others may be better able to. Perils face everyone in high office. You could, for example, sacrifice your prophethood on the altar of popularity. You must never relax your self-vigilance or fail to examine your motives.

R.D. Is there a danger of taking the burdens and responsibilities, big as they are, too seriously?

D.C. Yes, they could crush you if you couldn't let them go at the end of each day. Some lines from the hymn 'O my Saviour, lifted' have been of help to me.

> Bringing all my burdens,
> Sorrow, sin, and care,
> At Thy feet I lay them,
> And I *leave* them there.

61

If you can do that, you can wake up next morning ready to face the challenges again.

Stephen Neill in his book on the Ministry tells the story of a priest who was worried and overwrought. While praying one night, just before going to bed, he heard a voice say, 'Now, Quayle, you leave it to me. I'll stay awake.' You can keep your sanity and balance if you put all your trust in God.

R.D. In another of his books, *The Unfinished Task*, Neill writes of the dangers facing people in authority: especially pride and the twin delusions of power and self-reliance. He refers to them as spiritual dangers. During your years in high office did you have enough time for prayer and contemplation?

D.C. I was very fortunate to be able to worship every morning in the lovely chapel at Lambeth, before the arrival of the secretaries, the visitors and the daily post. The chapel was almost completely destroyed during the war and rebuilt in Geoffrey Fisher's day. Although I should have gone earlier to the chapel to prepare myself in private prayer, my time of worship there with close colleagues was priceless, and I couldn't have *begun* to do my job without it. Depending on the day's engagements, which inevitably interfered at times, I would also go to the chapel for Evensong.

R.D. It is often said that high office—indeed all leadership—is lonely. Was it?

D.C. Yes. After you have sought advice—as I repeatedly did—you have to decide whether to accept, reject or amend it. The same is true for prime ministers and managing directors. Eventually you have to make the final decision. Having done so, it is usually fatal to consider reversing it. You would then start to dither, and that would be no good for you or your colleagues or the organisation you are trying to serve.

R.D. Wavell said the very same thing about generalship: once you have made a decision, you must stand by it.

D.C. That reminds me of the story about the general whose battle plans were getting into a muddle. A bright young officer came along and said. 'General, I really think you ought to consult a computer about this.' Somewhat reluctantly, the general thought he had better get some objective advice, so he fed into the computer the question, 'Should we advance or retreat?' Within seconds, the answer came back, 'Yes'. This didn't help very much, so he fed in another question, 'Yes what?' And the answer came back, 'Yes, *Sir*'.

R.D. One of the most publicised events of your time at Canterbury was the 'Call to the Nation'. What are your reflections now on that initiative?

D.C. It was a combined call in 1975 made by the Archbishop of York and myself. In retrospect I am thankful for it. We felt strongly that the moment had come when such a Call ought to be given, without being delayed by the complications of making it ecumenical.

Although I see myself as one of the most ecumenical of men, I was aware that a nationwide Call has many built-in complications, and I felt this was one of those occasions when the established Church of the country had a right and a duty to act alone. We naturally told leaders of the other Churches and had their goodwill.

By the nature of this Call, the results were not easy to assess, nor could they be expressed in diagrams and statistics. That will never be possible. And yet some of the results were remarkable. Tens of thousands of people wrote to Lambeth: this in itself was an interesting phenomenon.

We posed two questions, 'What sort of society do you want—for yourselves, your children and your grandchildren?' and, 'What kind of people must we be if we are to achieve that sort of society?' At first sight, those questions may look simple, but they can go very deep if you are prepared to follow their implications. They got people talking about religion and about priorities. Is money being considered to matter more than people? Are material comforts being considered to matter more than principles?

Not only did religion again become a major topic of conversation all over the country, in pubs as well as universities, but hundreds of groups were formed, here and abroad, composed of Christians and non-Christians, to explore the questions we posed. And new opportunities were created for Christians to talk to the non-committed or the semi-committed about a wide range of issues affecting us all.

R.D. We've talked about the outward life of high office and also about the inward life. Is there anything else you would like to say about those nineteen years at York and Canterbury?

D.C. And before York, five years as Bishop of Bradford. I often thank God for the gracious way He has led me on: starting in the comparatively small diocese of Bradford, where I began to learn what it means to be a bishop, and then to the great Sees of York and Canterbury. Benson, by contrast, started at Truro and went straight from there to Canterbury. The Church of England and the Anglican Communion are complex organisations in structure and in procedures, and so I am profoundly thankful for the timing and progression of my appointments.

R.D. How do you feel now about the timing of your retirement?

D.C. In years past, Archbishops tended to die in office. Davidson retired when he was eighty and died a couple of years later. I can remember seeing him in Golders Green when I was about eighteen. Temple died in office—he was in his early sixties—after only two years at Canterbury, 1942–4. Fisher retired at seventy-five; Michael Ramsey and I at seventy.

I left when I did for two reasons. I was aware that at my age a man's powers can decline, and the quality of his work diminish, without his realising it, and perhaps not many people would have the courage to tell him.

There were also family reasons. I felt I owed it to my wife not to go on much past the age of seventy. In the light of the early months of my retirement, I don't regret my decision.

I was the last Archbishop not to come under legislation compelling him to resign at a specified age. From now on the Archbishop of Canterbury will have to resign at seventy, unless, for some special reason, he and the Sovereign agree he should have one more year in office.

R.D.   How are you managing the transition period?

D.C.   A lot of people say how difficult it can be. I have not found it too difficult, partly because I have a happy home, and partly because I have a lot to do.

I admit to some element of relief in not having to exercise ultimate responsibility in so many matters. One's ministry never ends, and I am now freer to plan ahead. Invitations keep coming in—to preach, to lecture, to travel, to speak with clergy, to write books—and I have to choose from among so many opportunities.

I am fortunate in still being able to meet a number of interesting and stimulating people. And I feel so grateful to God for the privilege of a continuing ministry, especially to clergy.

R.D.   If you could have your life all over again, what might you do less of and what might you do more of?

D.C.   Perhaps less administration, and more teaching. But admin is necessary and holy and a gift of the Spirit; and St. Paul includes administration as one of the gifts of the Spirit (Rom. 12, NEB). In the life and work of an archbishop, sound administration can be *ad majorem gloriam dei*—to the greater glory of God.

I would certainly want to do more praying, more thinking, more reading; more action and less activism. Too many lives have as their motto the words on cereal packets: 'Tear along the dotted line'. Too much time is spent dashing around at a fiendish speed and achieving little. I often warn clergy of the danger of thinking you do a service to God and your fellow-man by a great quantity of work rather than by concentrating on its quality.

R.D. And the danger of living, as it were, in the future, always working *towards* a goal, rather than being fully in the moment, aware of what *is*.

D.C. That's right. God is always to be found in the present moment.

4 JESUS

R.D. As you contemplate the nature and personality of Jesus, as you have done all your life, what are the characteristics that you find most appealing, most inspiring?

D.C. First, Christ's intimacy with the Father, the source of all. Writers such as Jeremias have commented on Christ's use of 'Abba', which St. Paul expounds in Galatians 4 and Romans 8. 'Abba' is close in tone to 'Daddy', 'Dear Father', and yet in the Lord's Prayer it is immediately followed by 'who art in heaven'. Here we have a deep and tender intimacy combined with respect and awe. This relationship is expounded in St. John—attributing to Jesus the saying: 'I do always those things that please Him' (John 8:29)—and also in the Synoptic Gospels.

Second, His love for people. He had compassion for the multitudes, spent much time in the training of the Twelve, and related deeply to individuals: the woman at the well (John 4); the woman with a haemorrhage who touched Him, not causing Him to recoil because she was regarded as unclean, but to rejoice to see her healed (Mark 5:25–34); the demoniac whom the chains could not hold, but who was held by the presence of Jesus (Mark 5:1–20); and the woman of ill repute (Luke 7:37, 38) who washed His feet with her tears.

R.D. He could vary His approach.

D.C. Yes, He had profound psychological insight. This was another characteristic. 'Do you *want* to be made whole?' He would ask, knowing how many people derive some gain from continuing to be ill. He dealt with people in a great variety of circumstances and had extraordinary penetration

67

and intuition into character. At the end of John 2 (verses 24–5) is the revealing comment: '. . . he knew all men, and needed not that any should testify of man: for he knew what was in man.'

I often turn that description into a prayer before someone comes to see me: praying that God will enable me to see beyond the opening words to the person's real needs, help him express and clarify those needs and discover his own solutions.

To stand before Jesus was to be confronted by enormous power and strength. This is the fourth characteristic I would select. '. . . thou hast had five husbands' (John 4:18): that must have felt like a verbal dagger-thrust, but Jesus restored her morale before sending her on her way. And when she entered the city she said, 'Come, see a man which told me all things that ever I did: is not this the Christ?' (John 4:29). His authority was complemented by gentleness.

An example of His resolute sense of destiny and direction comes after Peter's declaration (Matt. 16:22) of the Messiahship of Jesus in which Peter could not bear to include the prospect of Jesus suffering to the death. Jesus, sensing danger, then says, 'Get thee behind me, Satan. You are trying to hold me back from the Cross. You are a tempter.'

Believing in the humanity of Jesus, we can but assume that His was a progressive self-awareness. From the early days of His ministry, He must have been aware that trouble, danger, mockery and cruel death lay ahead. We have to read the Gospels with caution where they speak of the awareness Jesus had of His destiny, but it seems clear that Jesus was increasingly conscious of impending suffering. As to His self-honesty, we can see how strongly He resisted all temptation, and how open He was to emotions, even to the point of crying out, when dying on the Cross, 'My God, my God, why hast thou forsaken me?' (Matt. 27:46).

R.D.   What would you like to say about Jesus as teacher?

D.C.   Incomparable. As a poet (whose name I don't know) said:

He spoke of lilies, vines and corn,
The sparrow and the raven,
And words so natural yet so wise
Were on men's hearts engraven.
And yeast and bread and flax and cloth
And eggs and fish and candles,
See how the most familiar world
He most divinely handles.

The Gospels breathe the air of the hills of Galilee. Jesus had a gift for the parabolic method of teaching which quickens the imagination. He used imagery superbly well: sometimes a short brush-stroke such as in Matthew (13:24) at the beginning of a parable, 'The kingdom of heaven is likened unto a man which sowed good seed in his field', and later in the same chapter (verse 33) Jesus likens the kingdom of heaven to 'leaven, which a woman took and hid in three measures of meal, till the whole was leavened'; at other times the imagery is extended, such as the parable of the Prodigal Son (Luke 15), which I prefer to call the parable of 'the Two Lost Boys'.

R.D. Another aspect of His style is His use of irony, but perhaps one needs to know the period and its languages quite well to be able to sense when He was being ironic.

D.C. He was capable of puns: this is especially evident if you translate from the Greek into the Aramaic which He spoke. There is, for example, a lovely pun in Matthew (3:9): 'God is able of these stones (*abanim*) to raise up children (*banim*) unto Abraham.' I have in fact used the Hebrew here, but the Aramaic must have been near enough to this for the pun to have raised a chuckle from the crowd.

R.D. You said in *Prayers of the New Testament* that Jesus spent His ministry 'giving Himself away to sinners'; and Malcolm Muggeridge in a book about Mother Teresa wrote: 'There is much talk today about discovering an identity, as though it were something to be looked for . . . then hoarded and treasured. Actually, on a sort of Keynesian principle, the more it is spent, the richer it becomes.'

D.C. St. Paul in the great 'hymn' in Philippians (2:5–11) speaks of Christ Jesus who 'took upon him the form of a servant . . . humbled himself, and became obedient unto death, even the death of the cross.' Jesus instructed His disciples thus: 'He that findeth his life shall lose it: and he that loseth his life for my sake shall find it.' (Matt. 10:39). And Isaiah in the last of the four Servant Songs (chapters 52 and 53) contains the prophecy of His being 'wounded for our transgressions', His soul being 'an offering for sin'.

I met Mother Teresa in Bangladesh. She is a tiny, radiantly happy woman. In her conversation, a sense of beauty and love-for-all recur again and again like a refrain. She and the Sisters in her Order ease the last hours of the poor and the destitute, the starving and the abandoned. She owns little more than her clothes. She is a living illustration of someone who feels enriched through constant giving.

R.D. Also in *Prayers of the New Testament* you speak of the rhythm in the life of Jesus: His ability to alternate the activity of life in the market-place with solitude when He went alone to the hillside.

D.C. We are given enough hints of that in the New Testament to suggest a pattern. For example, before choosing the Twelve He spent a night in quiet prayer alone on a mountainside (Luke 6:12).

Nature has a lot to teach us: the ebb and flow of the tide; the cycle of winter, when the fields are fallow and receptive to snow, rain, sun and wind prior to the hope of spring, the ebullience of summer, and the autumn's harvest.

There is also the rhythm of our own daily life: the slowing-down of the body during sleep, in preparation for the coming day's activity.

We should use Nature's example as a model for absolute regularity in our own spiritual life. We cannot do without regular times of silence and prayer if, in our everyday contact with others, we aspire to be loving, creative, patient and healing.

R.D. You seem to be implying that Christ's outpouring of love was not a profligate spending of Himself; it was rooted in awareness of how much energy He had.

D.C. That's right. Of a day when Jesus was healing by touch and by word, Mark (5:30) tells us: 'Jesus, immediately knowing that virtue [healing power] had gone out of him, turned him about in the press and said, Who touched my clothes?' He was aware, in the moment, of the cost of giving. In any spiritual giving—be it preaching or healing or in listening at depth to someone in trouble—you feel some of your strength being drained away.

During a recent series of lectures in Washington D.C.—at the College of Preachers to mark their fiftieth anniversary—I spoke about nervousness in the pulpit. I said that anybody who really gives of himself when he preaches knows that something is happening to his adrenalin: his senses and sensitivity are heightened. This is a necessary concomitant of any creative activity; it is not the same thing as nervous anxiety, which can have an inhibiting, paralysing effect.

Christ had much to say in the Sermon on the Mount (Matt. 6:28–34) about the dangers of worry: 'Consider the lilies of the field, how they grow; they toil not, neither do they spin . . . Take no thought, saying What shall we eat? or, What shall we drink? or, Wherewithal shall we be clothed? . . . your heavenly Father knoweth that ye have need of all these things . . . Take therefore no thought for the morrow: for the morrow shall take thought for the things of itself.'

R.D. The other day I came across an interesting passage in J. B. Phillips's book *God our Contemporary*. He spoke of Christ's spiritual gift for concentrating on what is really essential, and then continues: '[He gives little explanation] of the human situation. He does not argue about the existence of suffering or evil, still less does He seek "to justify God's ways to man". He accepts it [the human situation] and He concentrates upon the centre . . . the human heart.'

71

D.C. It was more Greek than Hebrew to ask the question, 'Why?' The Greek question would be: 'Where does evil come from?' Jesus faces the fact of evil and asks: 'What can we do about it?' This was essentially a Hebrew approach.

In Luke (13:4–5) Jesus refers to the tower of Siloam which fell and killed eighteen people. Our Lord doesn't explain why it happened; all He says is that their death in this manner does not prove that they were more sinful than anyone else. That is a source of comfort to me: it indicates that suffering isn't necessarily proportionate to sin or the direct result of sin. But it still leaves me asking a great many questions.

R.D. Several of the sayings of Jesus puzzle me, and I'd be glad of your comments on them. Most, if not all, seem to show a sharp edge to his personality. For example, (Matt. 10:34): 'Think not that I am come to send peace on earth: I came not to send peace, but a sword.'

D.C. Here our Lord's Hebrew background is clearly seen. In order to understand Jesus, it is essential to understand the Hebrew language and mentality and way of seeing life. Sometimes Hebrews expressed result as if it were purpose. Occasionally we do this in English. For example: 'He was cold; he went indoors only to find that the temperature was still below zero.' He was hoping it might be warmer. The *result* of his going inside was to find it was still cold. Jesus was not saying that His purpose was to bring the sword. What he implied was: 'The result of my coming is, you will often find, not peace but contention.'

I'll give you another example of this grammatical device: '. . . a man and his father will go in unto the same maid, to profane my holy name . . .' (Amos 2:7). In fact the man and his son don't think about God when they indulge in an immoral act; their profaning of His name is the *result* of their behaviour.

R.D. What did Jesus mean here by His use of the word 'sword'?

D.C. The sword of division. For example, if one member of a family is a believer and the others are not, this will often lead to argument and dissension.

R.D. Dissension resulting from one person's decision? And the implication that a commitment to God would, in this case, entail less conformity to the ways of one's family?'

D.C. That's right.

R.D. This prompts me to ask you about the next two verses (Matt. 10:35–6): 'For I am come to set a man at variance with his father, and the daughter against her mother, and the daughter in law against her mother in law. And a man's foes shall be they of his own household.'

D.C. This is surely hyperbole. Jesus does not want me to hate any member of my family, but my loyalty to Him must be absolute, unswerving: if He makes clear His intention for me to work in another country, then abroad I must go—even if this means separation from one's parents.

R.D. Another puzzling passage is the cursing of the fig tree (Mark. 11:12–14). Here Jesus seems to have acted with impatience.

D.C. This is a puzzling one. The Evangelist says the season for figs had not yet come. The point of the story would have been clearer if it *had* been the time of year for figs and yet the tree wasn't yielding any. Presumably the story should be seen as parabolic, with the fig tree symbolising the unrepentant people of Israel.

Some of the seemingly harshest sayings and curses attributed to Jesus are to be found in St. Matthew. This raises the question: Are they the *ipsissima verba*, the exact words, of Jesus? The very raising of this question, without clear criteria, would put us on difficult ground: there would be a danger of our forming a picture of Jesus according to our own needs and expectations; and rejecting, as inaccurate reportage by the Evangelist, whatever doesn't fit that picture.

Jesus sometimes spoke in a grave, almost harsh, way in order to shake certain people into greater awareness. Paul talks of a conscience that has become hardened, calloused: he uses a medical word (2 Cor. 3:14; Eph. 4:18). Sometimes a callous has to be removed, scraped away. And when the emotional or spiritual life has gone stale, harsh measures are often the most effective treatment. This is true of individuals and of whole communities, and the teaching of Jesus must be seen in the challenge He presented to the society and mores of His day.

R.D. How do you interpret Luke 19:26–29: 'For I say unto you, That unto everyone which hath shall be given; and from him that hath not, even that he hath shall be taken away from him. But those mine enemies, which would not that I should reign over them, bring hither, and slay them before me.'

D.C. I have two comments. First, it is a parable. The essence of the interpretation of parable is not to pay too much attention to detail. Second, there *is* a stern element in the teaching of Jesus. There *is* judgment. There are eternal issues at stake. But His authority is not the authority of pride or power; it is the authority of love.

R.D. Lastly, the parable of the Unjust Steward (Luke 16:1–12) and those strange words (verse 9): 'Make to yourselves friends of the mammon of unrighteousness; that, when ye fail, they may receive you into everlasting habitations.'

D.C. This is a notoriously difficult parable. How can worldly wealth have anything to do with an eternal home, 'everlasting habitations'?

We sometimes read Holy Scripture too solemnly. After all, meaning depends on tone of voice as well as on the words that are spoken. Perhaps this is an ironic, almost cynical, utterance; the intended tone being, 'Take that and think it over! Just *imagine* it.'

R.D. In his autobiography *Memories, Dreams and Reflections*, Jung said that the imitation of only one side of Christ's nature is killing the Church: false piety causes many Christians to lose touch with the realities of faith.

D.C. If you look at a cross-section of books about Jesus, you'll see He has been described in every possible way, from social agitator to 'gentle Jesus, meek and mild'.

R.D. He is always more than our imagination can conceive.

D.C. Yes, He is so great and we are so small. We try to reduce Jesus to the scale of our own thinking.

R.D. Phillips sums it up perfectly in the title of his book *Your God is too Small*.

D.C. I'm sure that's right. We should be thankful for the range of the New Testament. Temple in his *Readings in St. John* speaks of the fourth Evangelist as the great interpreter of Jesus. Temple likens John to a portrait painter, and the Synoptists' pictures to photographers' snaps.

R.D. Christ died when He had barely reached middle age. What symbolic significance do you attribute to this? There is something archetypal in being killed during one's prime.

D.C. Isaiah's prophecy (chapter 53) of the sufferings and death of Christ speaks of Him 'cut off out of the land of the living' even though He 'had done no violence, neither was any deceit in his mouth . . . he hath poured out his soul unto death . . . and he bare the sins of many, and made intercession for the transgressors.'

Death at an early age is one of the mysteries of life. Alexander the Great, for example, also died in his thirties: his was an astonishing achievement of military might, as our Lord's was in a life of love. And death sometimes comes prematurely to those who have just reached high office. Temple had been at Canterbury for only two years. He was twice the age of our Lord, but why wasn't he given another few years? Pope John Paul I died only a few weeks after being enthroned.

This subject affected me with special poignancy after Lord Mountbatten and several members of his family were killed by terrorist bombing while on holiday. On the same day I conducted a burial service for a woman in her eighties and a boy in his early teens.

I hang on to the belief that in God's kingdom there is no waste. The body dies but the soul lives on, and those who have died continue to influence those who remember them.

R.D.   What is the symbolic significance of the fact that Jesus didn't marry?

D.C.   Jesus said (Matt. 19:11–12 NEB): '[Not to marry] is something which not everyone can accept, but only those for whom God has appointed it. For while some are incapable of marriage because they were born so, or were made so by men, there are others who have themselves renounced marriage for the sake of the kingdom of Heaven. Let those accept it who can.'

Our Lord had a real and deep affection for women but He must have sensed early on that His servant-Messiahship would have brought untold sorrows to a life-companion.

R.D.   Another aspect of His life—as a reading of Hebrews shows—is as a pioneer, forging a trail for us to follow. 'Tears and smiles like us He knew.' He knew at first hand the whole range of life's experiences. Whatever pain or difficulty we may have, we know that Christ shares our suffering.

D.C.   Yes, the Epistle to the Hebrews (4:15–16) gives the supreme exposition of Christ's humanity: 'For we have not a high priest which cannot be touched with the feeling of our infirmities; but was in all points tempted like as we are, yet without sin. Let us therefore come boldly unto the throne of grace, that we may obtain mercy, and find grace to help in time of need.'

The word you referred to—*archēgos*, a pioneer—can be used in the sense of a man who, having been shipwrecked, ties a rope round his middle and swims for the shore, so that he can be followed by other survivors. This word appears several times in the New Testament—such as in Acts 3:15 and 5:31, and Hebrews 2:10 and 12:2—and is used of our Lord in His supreme role as initiator, *the* way of salvation, the one who gives impetus to others.

R.D.   In Gospel narrative, how long is the gap in the description of the life of Jesus?

D.C.   We have very little material to work with. St. Luke says that Jesus began His public ministry when He was around thirty. We are told nothing about what have become known as 'the hidden years' apart from the famous story (Luke 2:41–52) of the trip to Jerusalem for the Feast of the Passover. Jesus was then twelve years old. He stayed on in the city. Joseph and Mary went back to find Jesus and saw Him in the temple, seated among teachers of the law, listening to them and asking questions.

This episode shows us how rapidly, in His adolescent years, the mind of Jesus was developing. Almost rebuking His parents He says—and this can be translated in one of three ways—'Didn't you know that I must be about my Father's business?' . . . 'in my Father's home?' . . . or 'among my Father's people?' Already His identification, His *total* loyalty to God, is clear.

The Gospels are silent about the life of Jesus from the time of His birth until this incident at the age of twelve; and from then until the baptism, the temptation, and the start of His public ministry. We long to peer into those hidden years. There are so many questions about which we can only speculate.

We can draw certain deductions from the way Jesus speaks in the parables: for example He mentions a single lamp which gives light to a whole house. Elsewhere we read His description of a woman kneading dough, and we can picture the young Jesus watching His mother in the kitchen. Presumably He is drawing on the memory of the simple home in which He and His family lived.

R.D. Knowing what we do about methods of transport at the time, what do you suppose might have been the longest of Christ's travels?

D.C. He went from the north—Nazareth, Galilee, Capernaum—to Jerusalem: a journey of two or three days by donkey, through countryside on the west of the Jordan. During the years of His public ministry He crossed the Jordan into the area of Decapolis, the ten towns, where Greek was spoken. Jesus was probably bilingual, speaking Aramaic as His mother tongue but fluent enough in Greek to enable Him to travel with ease on the eastern side of the Jordan. I suppose the limits of His travels would have been to Tyre and Sidon in the north; and to Jerusalem and the desert in the south, the kind of country where Amos came from. Beyond these geographical boundaries, His travels would have been in the realm of thoughts and prayers and creative imagination.

We have no evidence that Jesus ever travelled as widely as St. Paul did. Paul visited Asia Minor, going through what is now Turkey. He went to Rome and possibly to Spain. Jesus would have heard of similar journeys and been conscious of being in the midst of the Graeco-Roman world. When He read the Old Testament, He learned of other great civilisations, their rise and fall.

R.D. Because long journeys were at that time rare and thus worthy of note, presumably we can infer, from lack of mention of them in the Gospels, that Jesus lived and travelled within a limited area. Recently I was talking with a friend about this and 'the hidden years'. For her, it makes Jesus all the more credible, personal, and approachable, and enhances His living presence.

D.C. Jesus once said to His disciples, 'I am not sent but unto the lost sheep of the house of Israel.' (Matt. 15:24). He whose message is universal seems to have been content to live His life within a specific area: this is perhaps a spatial illustration of His self-emptying.

Thomas may have gone to India. St. Paul travelled throughout the Graeco-Roman civilisation. Before long, Christianity reached Gaul and Britain. There were British bishops at the Synod of Arles in the year 314, so the Church must have been founded here well before then.

Jesus founded a base, a community—local, specific, personal—from which His mind and Spirit could expand and ultimately reach out to the whole of mankind.

5   THE BIBLE

R.D.   What in your opinion are the strengths and weaknesses of the leading English versions of the Bible?

D.C.   This is a subject which has occupied me, as student and as teacher, from the age of sixteen when I began to learn Greek and Hebrew, all through my years as a teacher in Manchester, Canada and London, to my appointment as chairman of the New English Bible Joint Committee.

I had the privilege of meeting Moffatt in New York, having long admired his version, which was a great achievement. He did a few quirky things: such as calling the Ark 'a barge' and translating the introduction to chapter three of the book of Job: 'Eyob began: "Perish the day I was born, the night that said 'It is a boy!'"' His was a one-man version—in itself a considerable feat—and he helped many Christians by putting the Bible into the language of the people.

The Authorised Version was produced by half-a-dozen committees whose members in the end achieved quite a degree of homogeneity in their translation.

The New English Bible I have a special fondness for, but it has its weak points: I hope they find an alternative to their unintended *double entendre*, 'loose livers' (1 Cor. 5:9) in any future edition.

The New English Bible, like most modern versions, makes a clear differentiation between prose and poetry. By this method of setting out the type, passages of straightforward narrative can be contrasted with utterances of the prophets. As in Judges 5, we can even recapture something of the rhythm and pulse of Hebrew verse.

C. H. Dodd was *the* moving spirit in the work on the New English Bible. I heard him give one of his famous lectures on St. Paul towards the end of his distinguished professorship at

At home

Above left: Early days as a curate.
Above right: With the family at piano.
Left: Jean at Lambeth Palace.

The Anglican Communion

Above: New York 1976. *Below:* Presentation at General Synod, 1979.

With the people

Above left: Pastoral visit. *Above right:* Chatham dockyard pub 1976.
Below: Underground at a Kent Colliery, 1977.

[Foto Felici]

Canterbury and Rome

Above: With Pope Paul VI, Rome 1977. *Below left:* Exchange of gifts 1977, also in Rome. *Below right:* With Pope John Paul II at his inauguration, 1978.

[Foto Felt

[Gopal Chitra Kufeer]

Church ambassador

Above: Wreathlaying an Mahatma Gandhi's Memorial plinth, Delhi, 1976.
Below: With President Kenyatta at a reception, Nairobi, 1975.

[Ringolds A. Muziks]

Diverse Duties

Above: At the BBC. *Left:* The response to the Call the Nation, 1975. *Below:* Honorary degree ceremo Kent University, 1978.

Church and State

Opposite: above left: With Len Murray, 1977. *Above righ* With the Duke of Edinburgh, 1979. *Below:* With Ku Waldheim, Secretary-General of the United Nations, 197

[Press Association]

[Gerald J. Sharp]

[United Nations/M. Grant]

[*Kentish Gazette*]

National sorrow: national joy

Above: The funeral of Dowager Lady Brabourne and Nicholas Knatchbull 1979.
Below: The wedding of the Prince of Wales and Lady Diana Spencer.

Manchester. One day there will be a thorough revision of the New English Bible, but I feel sure that the basic work of Dodd and his team will remain.

Where do we go from here in our discussion on versions of the Bible of which there are so many?

R.D.   Phillips?

D.C.   There he was, Vicar of the Church of the Good Shepherd, Lee, finding that the message of the Pauline Epistles was not reaching many young people, so he started work on his own translation. His was an original mind, and his spiritual life was moulded by quite a lot of suffering.

Some of the new versions are rather banal; and some reflect a particular allegiance within the Church—you can detect immediately the theological outlook of the translator. That I don't like. The reader should not need to ask the question: 'What sort of churchmanship do the translators represent?' No, the important questions are: 'Is this version true to the original?' 'Is the English clear and of good quality?' and 'Can the reader feel the spirit of the text?'

R.D.   How do you regard the Jerusalem Bible?

D.C.   I preached from the Jerusalem Bible last night and have been using it, by way of change, for my daily readings. It is a fine translation and has excellent footnotes which I often refer to.

R.D.   If you had to choose one version for accuracy and one for aesthetic appeal, which would they be?

D.C.   I confess to being biased, having had a tiny share in the producing of it, but I would go for the New English Bible on both counts. The level of scholarship is high: you wouldn't expect otherwise with someone of Dodd's calibre watching over the project all those years.

Godfrey Driver's influence may prove to have been rather overpowering in the Old Testament, but his mind to the very end of his life was so alive and alert: his knowledge of ancient languages invariably lit up obscure passages in Job and elsewhere. He was a son of S. R. Driver, the Old Testament scholar who worked on the Revised Version. Together they spanned nearly a century of Biblical scholarship.

I was not one of the translators of the New English Bible. I served on the Joint Committee, and as chairman still do so. Our job was in part to act as a link between the translators and the group responsible for the quality and clarity of the English.

R.D. You mentioned the Jerusalem Bible and your current use of it for the sake of variety and freshness. How can we make our reading of the Bible a living experience, especially for the passages we have heard and read so often?

D.C. If I were a parent of young children, I would want them to come to know one version really well, particularly if they were in the habit of learning a few verses by heart each day. Later in life, reading from a variety of versions can be a help.

Having no chapel here in Kent, to whose daily worship I can go, is an enormous loss, and I am trying to adjust to it. At present I am reading from several different versions. I also glance at a commentary to keep my approach fresh, especially with very familiar passages.

If you are conversant with the languages, you can always go back to the original. Edwyn Clement Hoskyns in his *Cambridge Sermons* (published in 1938, a year after he died) said that you can bury yourself in a lexicon and arise in the presence of God. I often quote that to undergraduates who are doubtful of the value of studying the original languages of the Bible.

Some of the books we spoil by too much splitting up: we would do better to read them straight through, in order to get their conspectus. For example, to read the whole of St. Mark unhurriedly takes not much more than an hour. I and many thousands have been impressed and inspired by Alec McCowen's recitation of Mark's Gospel, and he never needs so much as a glance at the text.

At the other extreme we have the Pauline Epistles whose wisdom and glory are so concentrated. With them, it is wise to read only a few verses at a time, contemplating them deeply, and if possible turning them into a prayer.

Reading the Bible with an attitude of stillness is important as well as difficult: so many distractions obtrude. But getting cross with yourself makes things even worse. You should just relax and start again.

'. . . thou shalt love the Lord thy God with all thy . . . *mind*' (Mark 12:30) as well as with other parts of yourself, and so you should bring to your Bible-reading all the brainpower God has given you. Therefore you should welcome any light which scholarship, ancient or modern, can cast on scripture. All sincere scholarship comes from the Spirit of Truth, but beware those self-styled experts who, in the words of T. R. Glover (a classical scholar and the Public Orator at Cambridge when I was an undergraduate), are experts at cultivating fog and calling it reverence.

R.D.   In your book *Convictions* you said of the Bible that we too often fail to see it as a modern book or set of books.

D.C.   In some ways the Bible is antiquated. Parts of it date from a civilisation in which the wheel and the craft of writing were at an early stage of development. And St. Paul, I suppose, couldn't travel in winter-time because of storms over the Mediterranean: he had to wait for spring before he could set out. Boat and pony were his only means of travel.

The Bible may be old, even outdated, from, say, a scientific or a technological point of view, and yet an Old Testament story can come with the suddenness of a meteor, smiting your conscience, bringing eternal truth to the very depths of your being. Such is the everlasting inspiration of the Bible.

R.D.   We need to look to the Bible as present-day revelation, open for the meaning and message to speak to us now, in the midst of our doubts and struggles, our human relationships and our search for deeper faith.

D.C.   That's right: an openness of mind, not only to new aspects of higher truth but also to the will of God in all aspects of our life. Given that approach, your Bible reading will come alive.

R.D. What for you are the New Testament passages, chapters or books which you can return to again and again with un-dimmed enthusiasm and always learn something new?

D.C. I'm glad you put your question in the way you did. Earlier this week a young man asked me what my favourite verse is. That I cannot say, but seminal passages, seminal books—yes.

High on my list would be the Epistle to the Ephesians with its noble doctrine of the Church; that hymn of love in 1 Corinthians 13; the great discourses in John's Gospel, especially chapters 14–16 with the doctrine of the Paraclete, the Comforter, culminating in chapter 17, the high-priestly prayer of Jesus. This is only a random selection from untold riches.

I return again and again to Romans, a book that has altered the history of the world because in it St. Paul elaborates as nowhere else in his writings the awe-inspiring doctrines of sanctification and of justification by grace through faith. Romans is, as it were, the finished statue of which Galatians was the model. Paul was the supreme interpreter of Jesus. Paul inherited the grandeur that was Rome and the beauty that was Greece. When interpreting the life, the ideas and the teachings of Jesus the Palestinian, Paul brought to bear Graeco-Roman culture and civilisation, its language and ways of thought.

Paul has suffered the penalty of having been a man of vision. His thinking and his writings are on such a colossal scale that many people despair of coming to terms with him intellectu-ally or spiritually. Few of us are ready to take a view of the cosmos!

Paul is often depicted—largely through ignorance—as a narrow fuddy-duddy, an unsympathetic spoilsport. In fact Paul offers us the key to the door of a full and liberated life, the life lived in and through the Holy Spirit. And thus his theology *sings*. He goes to the heart of doxology, the praise of God—the very reverse of the misguided notion that being a Christian implies self-punishment and lack of joy. Paul says in effect: 'Be free. Open yourself to the will and wind of the Spirit, and God will guide you on the path of peace, truth and love.'

R.D.   As St. Teresa said, 'God deliver us from sullen saints!' What would you choose from the Old Testament?

D.C.   If you are limiting me to one area, I would have to go to the eighth-century Prophets: the passionate justice of Isaiah and Amos; Hosea's yearning, tender, wounded love. And the four great servant songs of Deutero-Isaiah which I believe were formative in the thinking of Jesus and the pattern on which He based His Messiahship.

R.D.   I'd be glad of your comments on the authenticity of the Apocrypha. And how important is the Apocrypha for a Christian seeking spiritual inspiration in the Holy Word?

D.C.   You have introduced subjects of considerable importance. The Roman Catholic Church regards the Apocryphal Books as an integral part of their Scriptures, and in recent years the Bible Societies have been printing what the Roman Catholics would call 'complete Bibles', that is to say with the Apocrypha added.

The position of the Church of England is to be found in Article Six of our Thirty-Nine Articles of Religion which deals with the 'Sufficiency of the Holy Scriptures for Salvation'. It speaks of the fact that Holy Scripture, the Old and New Testaments, 'containeth all things necessary to salvation'. Article Six then says: 'And the other books (as Jerome saith) the Church doth read for example of life and instruction of manners: but yet doth it not apply them to establish any doctrine.' It then gives a list of the books of the Apocrypha.

From the point of view of Bible scholarship, the books of the Apocrypha, or some of them, are of great importance, indeed essential, for a real understanding of the New Testament. Those of us who served on the New English Bible committees treated the Apocrypha with as much care as the other parts.

The Apocrypha tells of the crucial historical and doctrinal developments of the years when the books were written. Let me give you some illustrations, beginning from the historical perspective. The two books of the Maccabees describe the resistance movement of orthodox Jews against Gentile thought and manner of life. Loyal Jews felt that compromise would mean disloyalty and they were prepared to be murdered for their faith.

In those books of the Maccabees we are given glimpses of the growth of the Pharisaic movement. The Pharisees appear rigid and narrow in the Gospels, but theirs was a noble movement to begin with. The Pharisees stood for purity of Judaistic faith and practice, in contrast to the more compromising Sadducees. I remember an amusing quatrain:

> There once was a proud Sadducee
> A courtly time-server was he;
> Loved aristocracy, hated democracy,
> Went out with Gentiles to tea.

This readiness to consort with the Gentiles caused immense indignation among the Pharisees.

This was the period of the growth of the synagogue, a place not only for the preservation of the faith among Jews, but a centre to which a wider circle was also attracted: Gentiles who were no longer able to believe in polytheism could come and listen to Scriptures which told them of the one true God.

In regard to doctrine, we see in some of the Apocryphal books, especially the Maccabees, the desperate efforts of a people to achieve a theodicy, a justification of the ways of God towards mankind. If the prophets, they said, were right in preaching a God of love and of justice, then why did He allow His people to be murdered by the Gentiles?

This wrestling with the realities of life, and with what they believed about the nature of God, led to the development of a doctrine of the after-life: if you don't see justice in this life you'll see it in the next. Foreshadowed in non-Apocryphal books such as Daniel, we have in the Apocrypha the emergence of a doctrine of heaven and hell. For an understanding of the New Testament, this is of great importance.

Then there is the Wisdom literature, noble books such as the Book of Wisdom and the Book of Ecclesiasticus. 'Let us now praise famous men, and our fathers that begat us. The Lord hath wrought great glory by them.' (Ecclesus. 44:1–2). These well-known lines, so often heard at memorial services or anniversary occasions, are so typically Apocrypha. Fore-shadowed, for example, by Proverbs 8, in which wisdom is personified, the Wisdom literature of the Apocrypha formed a background from which Johannine doctrine emerged. This is of major importance for our understanding of the Christology of the New Testament, especially when we come to chapters such as St. John 1, Hebrews 1 and Colossians 1. These are seminal to our thinking about the person of Christ.

6 PREACHING

R.D. In your book *Sinews of Faith* you describe preaching as the overflow, the outcrop, of a person's religion. Would you like to expand that thought?

D.C. All preaching worthy of the name starts from a relationship with God, and all Christian preaching from a relationship with God in Christ. Amos could only preach about justice because he had a continuing vision of the God of justice. Hosea could only preach about God's love because he had a vision of—we might say, a relationship to—the God of love who had raised up the tragedy of Hosea's thwarted married life and made it into a gospel.

Our supreme model is the preaching of Jesus Himself. He did not lecture *de Deo*, 'from on high', with an academic detachment; He spoke of God as the highest reality in His life, sharing the intimacy of a Father-Son relationship. This is what gave the power, the cutting edge, to the preaching of Jesus. He beckons to us that we may enter into a similar kind of living relationship with the Father, and may preach and witness from that stance.

Having said all that, I am due to preach tomorrow. Twice!

R.D. In your book *On Preaching* you said: 'The ministry of the word in the life-work of Jesus, the teaching and preaching task, went hand in hand with the ministry of healing . . .' So for Christ the speaking and the doing were in harmony. He not only spoke the Word; He *lived* the Word, and the Word lived through Him.

D.C. This arises from the Hebrew concept of word: not, as we say, so much hot air, but in itself a deed. Goethe translates John 1:1 as: '*Im Anfang war die Tat*', 'In the beginning was the deed'. This is a wonderful insight by a German into Hebrew thought, mind and language.

As the Psalmist puts it (Ps. 147:15, 18): 'He sendeth forth his commandment upon earth: His word runneth very swiftly . . . He sendeth out his word, and melteth them: He causeth his wind to blow, and the waters flow.'

Christ's power to heal not only united word and work, it revealed His concern for the whole of a person's being. Take, for example, His healing of the paralytic brought to Him by four men (Mark 2:1–12). Jesus didn't lay His hands on him and say, 'Your paralysis is cured'. Jesus looked at him and said, 'Son, your sins are forgiven.' 'I am concerned', we might picture our Lord as saying, 'not primarily with your paralysis, although I feel deeply for your suffering. Deal first with your sin and you will become a whole man again.'

R.D. I wonder if you regret, as I do, that our society is being submerged by words; our feeling and sensitivity for language is being eroded.

D.C. Yes, the spoken word is being cheapened. In some households a radio or television, or both, are blaring forth all day, to the point when they are like water flowing over a stone: nothing is absorbed. So much is available at the turn of a switch. Gone are the days when several thousand people would travel to London to hear the preaching of Liddon or Spurgeon.

R.D. What did you mean, in your book *On Preaching*, when you wrote of 'the joyful tyranny'—what a splendid oxymoron—'of being a minister of the word'?

D.C. I had two things in mind. First, let's look at the tyranny. A parish priest has to give two sermons every Sunday to the same congregation. It is no good saying to himself, 'I'm feeling a bit stale this week'. Here is the tyranny, the sheer regularity of the need to preach.

There is, at the same time, a great joy to preaching. Bishop Winnington-Ingram, who ordained me, said to me, when he was in his seventies, 'I never mount the pulpit steps without thanking God for another opportunity.'

The Gospel—*evangelion*—means 'good news'. And it is *immense* good news, the vastness of which we can only begin to explore in our short life. So a preacher has ground for perpetual joy, infinite in depth and height, for exploration and exposition, for stretching his own and his congregation's mind and spirit.

A preacher should learn to speak not only from within his own experience but also to point beyond it, giving a vision of hills whose distant outline he can only just discern, enriched by the heritage of the Church down the ages. If he does that, then the joyful element of preaching, the *adventure* of faith, will always be available and will lighten and lessen the tyranny.

R.D. If, as you say, a preacher points beyond his own range of experience, this will surely allow more space and scope for those who hear him to receive the message of the Holy Spirit in their own way and according to their own needs. To be too clear, too sure, too precise, is to limit the effectiveness of one's material. Hence the value of myth, allegory and parable.

D.C. Yes, I'm sure you are right. God enables the words of the preacher to be heard in different ways by different people. This is a form of miracle, and it shows the importance of the congregation: preaching is an activity of the whole Church, not just of the person in the pulpit.

This element of participation is missing for someone who talks or performs on radio or television. Just as an audience in a concert hall boosts the creativity of a musician, so the people of God contribute to the preaching of the Word. I often remind lay people of this by saying: 'The part you play in a sermon, while you sit in receptive silence, is *most* important. You will have knelt, I hope, before the start of the service, and asked God to bless the preacher. If, in addition, you pray for him during the course of the sermon, with your ears and mind and heart and whole being open to the word and truth of God, you are creating an atmosphere in which His word can flourish.'

R.D. How soon can you sense whether the congregation is truly worshipful?

D.C. Preaching can sometimes feel like a game of fives: your words keep coming back from the opposite wall; nothing else seems to be happening. But being human and fallible and liable to pride, your feelings may be misleading; God the Holy Spirit may have been at work in ways unknown to you.

At other times, preaching seems more like musician and audience, a mutually giving experience. How soon you can sense such an atmosphere from the pulpit varies greatly.

Some congregations don't settle down until you've done some introductory spadework. A minor battle goes on, during which some of the people say to themselves: 'He's a strange-looking chap' or, 'Hasn't he got a peculiar voice' or, 'He seems to be reading from notes'. The art is to guide them beyond such extraneous matters. The opening is all-important: you have to win their attention, lest they drift off to sleep or worry about the size of their rates bill or wonder what to cook for Sunday lunch.

So much depends on what has been done before you arrive, and on whether the soil has been dug, prepared and enriched. A prayerful congregation has learned about the Word, has learned about the sacraments, and about spiritual receptivity.

R.D.   What advice would you give to a preacher going through a dry patch?

D.C.   This is a time when your faith, your self-discipline and your prayer-life are tested, especially if you are very tired. You must go on, believing that God will bring comfort and support. Long before you kneel down to pray, He is waiting and available, ever ready to love and forgive.

R.D.   What are the marks of effective and really God-centred preaching: preaching which can meet the deepest needs and soothe, heal, challenge, encourage, strengthen?

D.C.   We have a model in our Lord's stimulation of mind and imagination as a route to the will of man. This is one of the main functions of preaching.

Jesus made the most skilled use of illustration. His parables are marvels of clarity, dealing with one point, one moral, at a time, enabling each to be firmly registered in the minds of his listeners. I used to suggest to my students that the difference between effective and ineffective preaching can be likened to a Bond Street shop window and that of a branch of Woolworth's. A Woolworth's window is—or used to be—crammed with dozens of articles. A Bond Street shop, by contrast, will feature a single hat, lit up against a black background. Many passers-by will covet such an attractive hat and even make sacrifices in order to buy one.

I usually find myself making three main points in a sermon, but I sometimes wonder if I might do better to make just one, especially in an age when, as you said, we are subjected to too many words. A poet once wrote: 'Who keeps one end in view makes all things serve.'

R.D. Perhaps a tendency to try to convey too much is a special danger of the early years of priesthood.

D.C. Yes, you pack in everything from the Creation to the Second Coming, and then wonder what you have left to talk about next Sunday! This is the work of an over-anxious amateur. But some men, long in the ministry, still haven't learned this lesson.

Someone once said that the best way to preach is to have a good beginning and a good ending and to keep them close together. A good beginning is vital: you capture or lose your listener in the first three minutes. And when you come to the end—finish. Don't drag on. Too many sermons resemble the saying: 'My little pet dormouse, his body is small but his tail is enormous.'

R.D. What are some other important aspects of the technique of preaching?

D.C. A preacher's theme is the drama of the Bible and of the spiritual life, the greatest drama of all time. Dorothy Sayers rightly said that many people have a wrong picture of Jesus: he was sharp, piercing, penetrating, never dull. Although a preacher shouldn't be histrionic, drawing attention to himself, he can still learn much from the actor's art: use of pause, clarity of diction, range of tone and expression. Also, most of us, in and outside the pulpit, speak too fast. We don't allow enough time for our message to be absorbed.

Preaching is a dangerous profession: there is often a subtle hope for approval; and an ever-present temptation to magnify yourself instead of your Master. Paul said that we should 'preach not ourselves, but Christ Jesus the Lord' (2 Cor. 4:5).

Every human personality is unique, a divine gift. Personality is an essential part of preaching, so long as we entrust it to God to use, and perhaps even heighten, in His own way, for His own purpose.

R.D. Do you look back on a service in an analytic way, trying to find at which points you might have said more or said less or guided the service in a different way?

D.C. I don't do much of that, but I have come home and said to my wife, 'I think I could have done much better.' I will be aware of having tackled an enormous theme and of not doing it justice; I will have made a great truth look small. To what extent have you magnified Christ—this is the touchstone of success or failure in preaching.

R.D. As you look back, are there any particular topics of Christian life or Christian doctrine, or passages from the Bible, that all through your preaching ministry you have come back to again and again, and can usually find something more to say about?

D.C. That question might be easier answered by someone whose ministry had taken him to only two or three parishes over a period of twenty or thirty years. Mine has been a peripatetic ministry ever since 1937 when I went to Canada to teach and visited the parishes of many of my students.

Through all the years of my three bishoprics I preached at a different church or cathedral almost every Sunday. I can remember one welcome exception to all this moving around. A tour I had planned did not take place, and so I was able to preach at a church in Maidstone on five consecutive Sundays. This was a splendid opportunity to offer the same congregation a series of themes with some continuity between them. The first four were entitled 'Who am I?', 'Who is God?', 'Who is Jesus?' and 'What about the Church?'. On the final Sunday I answered—from the pulpit—questions that had been sent in.

For sermon material I come back again and again to the person, the nature, of Christ; to the Pauline books such as the noble passages in Philippians 2 and Colossians 1; to the great and inexhaustible Johannine themes, especially the doctrine of the Word and the 'I am' octet—'I am the true vine . . . the good shepherd . . . the bread of life' and so on; to the Prophets; and to the Trinitarian concept of the Christian faith—the fatherhood of God, the person of Jesus, and the Holy Spirit, the Paraclete. This concept is so beautifully illustrated in the words of the Grace: 'The grace of our Lord Jesus Christ, the love of God, and the fellowship created by the Holy Spirit.'

R.D. Have you been aware of changes or evolutions in your style of preaching?

D.C. When, for example, I am instituting a new minister to a parish, and if I happen to know the man himself and the needs of the area, I have tended in recent years to become more conversational with a congregation.

R.D. We are treating the vocation to preach with the seriousness it deserves. I wonder none the less if you can recall any amusing or unusual incidents that have occurred during a sermon or other parts of a service?

D.C. I remember a rather embarrassing occasion in Montreal many years ago. I went up into the pulpit and placed my Bible and a few pages of notes on the little reading stand. The stand was too low, and I managed to heave it up, only to find it coming loose from its socket and tipping my Bible and my notes into this highly respectable congregation. A tail-coated gentleman picked up my belongings and handed them to me. I've laughed about that many a time.

There was another memorable occasion, this time when I was a curate in Islington. As I was reading one of the Lessons from a lectern placed in the centre aisle of the church, a very poor man came up to me and tugged at the sleeve of my surplice. He then walked out. Having no idea what this meant, I asked my churchwardens at the end of the service. They said he sold meat for cats in the market and in the streets, and that pulling on my surplice was his way of saying 'I'm sorry, I have to leave now and get on with my work.'

I got to know this man quite well and visited him and his family in their home. They were very poor. On a table were two plates bearing Hebrew characters. Being interested in Hebrew, I asked about the plates, where they had been bought and so on. He insisted on giving me the plates, one of the most touching gifts I've ever had in my life.

R.D. Have you ever made an amusing Freudian slip during a sermon?

D.C. Occasionally I have made a Spoonerism. When I am very caught up in a theme I am propounding, I tend to gain speed. As in driving a car, speed in speech can be dangerous. In the excitement of the moment, I sometimes make a slip of the tongue, but I can't recall any in particular.

R.D. Can you recall any slips while listening to a sermon either before or after you entered the ministry?

D.C. One of my sadnesses is that I am able to hear very few sermons. One of my heroes in the world of preaching is James Stewart, a Scottish divine who was Professor of New Testament at New College, Edinburgh. He wrote a marvellous book *A Man in Christ: Vital Elements of St. Paul's Religion* (1935), and his sermons live even when collected together in book form. How compelling are the very titles of these books: *The Strong Name*, *Heralds of God*, *King For Ever*, *The Wind of the Spirit*. Given the time, I would go a long way to hear a man of his calibre preach.

R.D. You were talking earlier about the help of preaching to a responsive congregation. Have you been to churches in which the people responded with Amens or other vocal affirmations that they were participating with you?

D.C. Yes, sometimes a mild joke brings a ripple or burst of laughter. Some people object to this: they say that church-going is too solemn and important a matter even for the occasional laugh. I don't agree. A chuckle or even a guffaw can indicate a release of tension, the opening of a person to receive deeper truths. Shakespeare brings a fool or a clown on to the stage every so often, and then, having given the audience some light relief, he returns to his major themes. Shakespeare knew a thing or two about the way into the human mind. And I'm sure you could give me some illustrations from works of music where the composer introduces a short *trio* or *capriccio* in the middle of a more serious movement.

We are made in such a way that we cannot stay in a state of tension or high seriousness for too long. Our Lord Himself had a good sense of humour. Imagine the wry smiles on the faces of his listeners when Jesus exclaimed: 'Ye blind guides, which strain at a gnat and swallow a camel' (Matt. 23:24). His humour often expressed itself in irony: 'It is easier for a camel to go through the eye of a needle than for a rich man to enter into the kingdom of God' (Matt. 19:24). One of the best examples of His lightness of touch is when He said: 'But whereunto shall I liken this generation? It is like unto children sitting in the markets, and calling unto their fellows, and saying, We have piped unto you, and ye have not danced; we have mourned unto you, and ye have not lamented' (Matt. 11:16–17).

Whatever method of expression Christ chose, His purpose was always to penetrate the defences of the self-satisfied and the complacent. He stimulated the imagination of His listeners as a way of entering into their conscience and their will.

Christ varied both His tone and the content of His message according to the nature of the audience. How the scribes and Pharisees must have squirmed in their shame and discomfort when Christ denounced them (Matt. 23) for their preoccupation with the law and ritual and outward show. He knew how to get under the skin of a sophisticated listener, an intellectual, just as He knew what imagery to use in order to reach the people of the countryside, the tillers of the land and the craftsmen. And T. W. Manson in his important book *The Teaching of Jesus* shows how Jesus distinguished carefully—without loss of spontaneity—between the way He spoke to and taught His disciples, the few, and the way He addressed the multitudes.

R.D. How often in your preaching do you spontaneously find a new word, a new phrase, a new way of expressing your ideas? Such an experience must truly be a gift from the Spirit.

D.C. Having done my preparation, I take to the pulpit an outline of what I want to say. Then during the sermon an incident, an illustration, from the previous week may occur to me, something which as I mounted the pulpit steps I had no idea I was going to mention. Perhaps in all forms of human communication we ought to be open for this to happen.

Preaching is a function of the Holy Spirit, using a narrow, fallible channel. You must not insult the Holy Spirit by not preparing, because the Spirit can inspire you at your desk as well as when you are in the pulpit. Nevertheless, you should try to remain flexible and open, leaving space for a word from above.

R.D. We were talking recently about television. The other day I read an article from a New York correspondent of the *Sunday Times* under the headline 'Praise the Lord and pass the TV guide'. He tells of the hundreds of radio and television stations in America which specialise in religious broadcasting, and their rapid growth in the past ten years. The fund-raising they do is enormous: 1,500 million dollars in 1979.

D.C. I can't speak from deep experience but I have seen and heard some of these programmes. Some of them seem to me to be a commercial prostitution of religion.

R.D. And yet, if the opportunities are sensitively used, religious broadcasts can be of help and comfort, especially to the aged and the housebound.

D.C. When I speak on radio or television, I utter the word of God to the best of my ability and trust the Spirit to make use of my efforts. I sometimes get letters which show how God has blessed what has been said in the form of comfort or challenge.

I feel sure that St. Paul, were he alive today, would accept every possible opportunity to broadcast in the service of the gospel. He made use of the one medium available to him: letters to specific areas as well as circular letters, encyclicals, sent by messengers on foot, boat and donkey. Copies could only be made by hand. How thankful Paul would have been for the work of Caxton and the pioneers of radio and television.

R.D. Have you been active in encouraging ministers to become effective in religious broadcasting?

D.C. Just north of London, at Bushey, is the C.T.V.C.— the Churches' Television Communications Trust—where lay-people as well as clergy train to make the best possible use of appearances on radio and television. I commend the work of this teaching centre.

R.D. I'd like to hear about your links with the College of Preachers in Washington D.C.

D.C. Many years ago when I was in Canada, I led a series of courses on preaching. This was a stimulating experience for me and, I hope, of use to clergy. I also went, first as an observer and then as a lecturer, to the College of Preachers in Washington, near that city's magnificent Cathedral. Recently, for their fiftieth anniversary, I made a return visit and gave some lectures.

Here in England about twenty years ago, a group of us— clergy as well as laity, all deeply concerned about the ministry of preaching—began to hold conferences for priests and Readers, and including some of our Free Church colleagues. They can hear themselves on tape, see themselves on video, submit sermons for comment, and be introduced to some of the more important books about preaching. One of the key figures behind this training was Prebendary Douglas Cleverley Ford, author of many books on preaching, but he had to cut down this particular work when he joined my staff at Lambeth.

R.D. Have you, in this country or in North America, helped women who want to preach?

D.C. Some women have come to my lectures at the College of Preachers in Washington, and some deaconesses-to-be attended my courses in Canada. I hope some women have read my books on preaching. I wish I could have done more.

R.D. I wonder if there are any special qualities which women can bring to the art of preaching?

D.C. Since the word 'sex' is linked to the word 'section' (both being derived from the Latin *secare*, to cut), we will only have a complete manifestation of the potential of preaching if both sexes contribute to the declaration of the Christian gospel.

I had the pleasure of admitting my wife as a Reader in the York Diocese. There are more women Readers now, which is a good thing, but still not enough of them. I agree with you—there are many special insights which a woman can bring to preaching, and we are impoverished if we don't hear them often enough.

R.D. Lastly, perhaps you would tell me a bit about your recent lectures in Washington D.C.

D.C. In the first of the three I gave a short survey of the past fifty years. In 1930 Herbert Hoover was President, and George V our Sovereign. Cosmo Gordon Lang had been at Canterbury a couple of years, and William Temple at York for one. Niebuhr was writing in America, and Dodd over here. These two men inspired the line: 'Thou shalt love the Lord thy Dodd with all thy heart and thy Niebuhr as thyself.'

The next lecture was a Bible study on the Holy Spirit and the preacher. And the last was an examination of the fruit of the Spirit (Gal. 5:22–3) in relation to preaching.

From time to time I feel I have nothing more to contribute to the theory of preaching and just continue with the practice of it. Then someone writes and asks me to give a lecture or a course of lectures, and I sit back and find that after all there is something new to say. Preaching is so vast a subject and so demanding a vocation that, as life goes on, you are bound to find new angles, new dimensions.

7 THE CHURCH

R.D. In *Stewards of Grace*, published in 1958, you spoke of the 'noise and superficiality which characterise so much of our contemporary society' and you referred to our 'frightened world'.

D.C. The dangers of devastating war come closer every year, as more and more, and ever-larger armaments are stock-piled. The peace, such as it is, is precarious, the result not of a spirit of co-operation but of mutual fear. A Damocletian sword hangs over the head of our whole civilisation. No wonder people of all ages are frightened.

In addition, scientific and medical advances are giving us a power over life and death which ethically we are probably not wise enough to use. This highlights the difference between knowledge and wisdom. Paul in his writings so often uses the word *gnosis*, knowledge, with a touch of unease: knowledge puffs up; love builds up (1 Cor. 13:2–4). Sometimes he prefaces the word with *epi*: *epignosis* is not accumulated intellectual knowledge; it is a divine gift—knowledge which perceives truth.

R.D. Another feature of our times is the widespread challenge to authority: not only to parents, teachers, political leaders, governments and institutions, but also to ultimate authority, spiritual authority.

D.C. You have pinpointed one of the main dangers of atheistic communism. If the leadership is corrupt, woe betide the people; there being no sense of ultimate authority, of divine judgment.

R.D. I fear also for our loss of continuity of values, our weaker grasp of the metaphysics of life and death and sexuality.

101

Perhaps the rate of change is such that many people are losing hold of the dimension which transcends all change.

D.C. I agree. Education is veering too far towards the scientific and the functional. Young people need more of a balance in their curricula: more history, more of the arts.

R.D. Another characteristic, especially of my generation, is the interest in all forms of the occult and esoteric knowledge.

D.C. Mankind is made apocalyptically. That body of Judaeo-Christian literature which we call 'apocalyptic' is an attempt to answer the questions: 'What is beyond this life?' and 'What is man's ultimate purpose?'. Apocalypse is the unveiling of what is to come. Its language—from Daniel and parts of the Apocrypha to the book of Revelation—is rich in symbolism.

The persecution of the Maccabees led to an early but strong doctrine of an after-life. There are hints of this in Daniel (12:2–3): 'And many of them that sleep in the dust of the earth shall awake, some to everlasting life . . . And they that be wise shall shine as the brightness of the firmament; and they that turn many to righteousness as the stars for ever and ever.'

Every one of us is born with the question inside us: 'What lies beyond?' It is part of our *humanum* to ask ultimate questions. Do my mother and Hitler have the same ultimate end? Does it matter what you do or fail to do in this life? Is there an after-life? Or was Bertrand Russell right when he said, 'When I die, I rot'? These are what I mean by apocalyptic questions which, just because we *are* humans, we ask. Those who don't seek the answers in the great world faiths seem to be looking to the realm of the occult.

R.D. From what we have been saying, it would seem that the Church has never before had a greater opportunity to offer insights into life's deeper meaning and purpose. How would you describe the changes in mood and morale of the Church in this country during your lifetime?

102

D.C. This is a profoundly difficult century for the Church, not only in England but all over the world. Many questions were asked in the trenches during the First World War, in the homes of the bereaved, and by the many men who returned to find not a country 'fit for heroes to live in' but a country of misery, poverty and mass unemployment. Then, only twenty years later, the world was again convulsed by war. These tragic experiences placed large question-marks against the doctrine of the perfectibility of man and against God Himself: Does He exist at all? If so, is He a God of love?

Another set of problems was caused by industrialisation, the growth of large conurbations, the wresting of man from his roots in open country, precipitating him into a concrete city, noisy, artificial and impersonal. Someone once said, 'The Church has not lost the working classes; it has never had them.'

Instead of a family growing up in a village where pub and club and church were all part of the life of the community where they would work, marry, have children and be buried—instead of that we have a highly mobile population with no deep roots, with no pattern of worship in the rhythm of every week. The local vicar thus has a constant struggle to build up and maintain his congregation.

We have not been adept at producing a generation of people who know their science as well as their theology. A narrow religious viewpoint has led to unnecessary conflict with science. All truth, after all, emanates from God. We need more men such as the present Bishops of Durham and Birmingham, John Habgood and Hugh Montefiore. They are at home in both spheres of knowledge.

As I see it, then, the Church in this century has been—and still is—wrestling with a whole series of questions: ethical, sociological, philosophical and theological.

R.D. New biographies have renewed interest in Thomas Merton. He once wrote: 'We too often forget that Christian faith is a principle of questioning and struggle before it becomes a principle of certitude and of peace. One has to doubt and reject everything in order to believe firmly in Christianity.' How open is the Church to preaching not only the good news but also the doubts, difficulties and struggles of the religious life? Unless the Church is honest about the dark side of man, those who are looking at us from the sidelines will say, 'I don't feel I am good enough to join you.'

D.C.   While you were reading that Merton quotation, I began thinking of Thomas in the Gospels, one of the most maligned of the Apostles, but one for whom I have deep sympathy. 'Let us also go, that we may die with him' (John 11:16). There is bravery and loyalty for you. He had seen enough of the majesty of Jesus to be prepared to go with Him, against all rational advice, to the centre of danger in Jerusalem.

Thomas struggled to find faith. He would never accept a creed, a belief, a statement, without questioning it. And our Lord dealt tenderly with Thomas, though with an occasional rebuke: '. . . blessed are they that have not seen, and yet have believed' (John 20:29).

I am sure what you said about the importance of honest questioning is right. Perhaps this is partly a matter of temperament: William Temple, for example. Bishop Paget of Oxford refused him ordination in 1906 because of his difficulty over the doctrine of the Virgin Birth. Temple was ordained two years later by Archbishop Davidson in Canterbury Cathedral. His was a questioning faith, though I don't think there was ever a period in Temple's life when he doubted the existence and fatherly governance of God.

We ought to be thankful for those who raise questions and don't claim to have all the answers. It can be a great relief to admit in public how narrow is the range of human understanding.

R.D.   What are some of the other stumbling-blocks about the Church for the non-believer? I'm thinking, for example, of the scandal of the divisions within the Church.

D.C.   Yes, I believe people often say, 'You talk about reconciliation. Well, become reconciled among yourselves and then I'll listen to you.'

Another problem is that some of our services are dull, lacking *life* and a sense of joy.

At a deeper level, many are unsure about the quality of our discipleship. A hypocrite, according to Greek derivation, is a play-actor. Most people are shrewd enough to perceive if we are play-acting or if we have a living experience of God.

This week I have been talking with clergy in Sussex. Their Bishop, Peter Ball, is a monk. He lives a life of total simplicity. I was told that the boys of a near-by school are impressed by his witness, his sincerity, and his natural sense of humour. They know he is not play-acting. They can see he is a man of prayer.

R.D.   John Robinson speaks of our age as a 'time of crucial divide' for the Church, and of our 'modern religious wilderness'.

D.C.   John has a gift for encouraging people to ask important questions. He is a fascinating combination: a radical mind, always seeking a new synthesis, and a man who has reached some very conservative conclusions, such as his early dating of the entire new Testament. *Honest to God* did not raise anything especially new, but coming from a bishop, and published in paperback, it set people talking about the faith.

The Church is foolish if it engages too rapidly or too thoughtlessly in a heresy hunt. We must allow our theologians to explore the frontiers of knowledge and of faith. This is part of their profession.

One of the most interesting examples of such exploration clashing with the orthodoxy of the Church was provided by Bishop Barnes of Birmingham. His son, Sir John, a retired diplomat, has recently published an absorbing biography, *Ahead of his Age*, of this remarkable Bishop, pacifist, teacher, mathematician, an ever-enquiring mind.

R.D. You were talking a moment ago about the Bishop of Lewes who is a monk. Ten years ago in York, Michael Ramsey suggested that the Christian Church was concentrating too much on the social gospel and, in so doing, had 'failed to be contemplative enough'.

D.C. I am sure that is true. Life is moving at a terrifying speed; unfortunately many Christians live at the same speed.

Peter Ball told me that he rises every morning at half-past four to pray. This gives him an hour and a half for prayer and contemplation before he joins his brothers for the first office of the day. Here surely is one of the reasons for the quality of his life.

The world is rushing to the point of exhaustion: over-population; depleting natural resources; not bridging the gap between rich and poor. The world aches in its need for serenity at the heart of daily life.

The rhythm of the life of Jesus is our model. For Him, prayer and activity were interwoven. He maintained inner peace amid the pressures of the crowds and the giving of His strength in healing, preaching and teaching. Jesus is our ideal of balance. People instantly recognise a person whose thoughts, words and actions stem from a calm centre.

R.D. The motor-car has revolutionised the way people spend their free time at weekends. Increased job mobility weakens parochial ties. Congregations have been shrinking year by year, and many more people believe they can live a godly life without going to church regularly. Do you see any hopeful signs of renewal in the Church of England?

D.C. When I did the rounds as a diocesan bishop I visited many churches with a lively sense of worship and social concern. I had to battle with those sections of the media which depict the Church as dying.

I found lively services, in which young and old members of the laity participate—the people of God in active co-operation. I found lively clubs and lively study groups.

The rising number of ordinands is another good sign, and a number of universities have flourishing theological faculties. Some of the young men and women want to be ordained, some want to teach religious knowledge in schools, and others feel that a study of theology will give an extra dimension to life, whatever they decide to do after leaving university.

The religious communities are another sign of growth. They are attracting people who want to make a lifetime commitment, and they provide a setting to which people of all ages and backgrounds come, for a time of quiet and for spiritual refreshment.

And if you look in any bookshop, or at any church bookstall, you will see that religious publishing abounds and flourishes. I have touched on just a few signs of hope for the Church; there are many others.

R.D. At a time when church attendance is not as strong as it was, every new edition and every new version of the Bible sells in tens of thousands.

D.C. Some churches in this country are increasing their membership, and of course new editions of the Bible have a world market. There are still people who believe, as I do, that you cannot be a reasonably educated and informed person, Christian or not, without possessing a copy of the Bible and having a good knowledge of its contents.

I mentioned a moment ago the growing number of groups of all sizes who meet regularly for prayer and Bible study. This is one of the most encouraging signs of the Seventies and Eighties and partly accounts for the continuing high sales of the Bible.

R.D. If you were to prepare a blueprint to ensure the future of the Church, what are some of the issues—I am sure Church unity would be one—the Church needs to work hard at in the next ten or twenty years?

D.C. I would certainly place Church unity high on my list. Secondly, we are only just beginning to answer the question:

What do we really believe about the function of women in the Church?

We also have some hard thinking to do about leisure, because, in addition to all those who are unemployed, we are rapidly moving towards a four-day or three-day working week. We need to combine Christian insights with those of education and sociology in order to offer people creative ways of spending their free time. Unless we help and train them to do something useful for their own community, as well as for other countries, we shall be in deep trouble.

The Church has a role in helping people to think globally and not insularly. We *do* live in a global village, and I am sad when I come across resistance by some parents to let their young people go abroad on missionary or temporary voluntary service. They fear this might spoil their children's career structure.

Here at home we have to do everything possible to help build a multi-racial society in which people of all races, creeds, and ages live together in harmony and are prepared to learn from each other.

R.D.   When you were at Canterbury you had two prisons in your diocese: one in Canterbury and one in Maidstone. What scope do prisons offer for more outreach by Christians?

D.C.   The Church can contribute to the discussion of a whole range of questions. Who should be imprisoned and for how long? Can the prisoner be given work which would serve as reparation for his wrong-doing? How can society adapt so that when a man leaves prison he can become a useful citizen?

R.D.   I also had in mind the regular visiting of prisoners and more support being given to their families.

D.C.   Already there is much fine work being done by our prison chaplains and by voluntary visitors. Burgon Bickersteth, who died recently, did such work. The fact that he came from a privileged background proved to be no barrier: he befriended a wide circle of people who had been in trouble with the law.

Another example is Irene Say, wife of the present Bishop of Rochester, who devotes a lot of her time to voluntary prison work. Much of it is uphill work, and there is a lot more to be done.

R.D. We were talking earlier about Church unity. Partly because of the controversy about women in the ministry, there are some Anglicans who say we are faced with a choice of moving towards Rome or towards the Free Churches, but that to try to move towards both simultaneously would be difficult, if not impossible. What are your feelings about this?

D.C. You have raised a difficult and challenging subject. The Anglican Communion has always thought of itself as a bridge Church, and we would do well to keep that image before us.

Ecumenism is probably easier away from one's home when we consider Churches which we rarely see! It is easier, for example, to talk about unity with the Orthodox Church than with the Methodists because the Methodist chapel is just down the road, while we rarely meet an Orthodox Christian!

Important conversations are being held between the larger Free Churches and Roman Catholicism, as there are between ourselves and Roman Catholicism. I long that we should do all possible, however difficult the task, to be a bridge Church.

R.D. What else about Anglicanism is most dear to you?

D.C. In Anglicanism I see two main features: first, catholicity—the historic continuity going back *long* before the Reformation; and second, evangelical zeal with roots deep in scripture. Anglicanism is at its best when these two elements are kept to the fore.

Another strand in our history, and one of enduring value, is our respect for scholarship and our openness to new intimations of truth. For all my occasional impatience with the Church of England, these strands bind me to the Church and make me thankful to be one of its members.

Lesslie Newbigin, one of the great leaders of the Church in South India, who writes so stimulatingly about inter-Church relationships, reminds us not only of our catholic and evangelical roots but also of our need for a charismatic element in an ecumenical Church. He did this as long ago as 1953 in his book *The Household of God*, before the full force of the charismatic movement burst on us. He was right. Read 1 Corinthians 12. Read Romans 12. We need a sensible charismatic element to vivify the Anglo-Catholic and the evangelical.

R.D. In your Lichfield Divinity Lectures of 1972 you said that 'the concept of the Church as a kind of general improvement society is scarcely that of the New Testament. Its task goes far deeper than that, precisely because man's need goes far deeper than that.'

This leads me to want to ask you about Church and State, and Church and politics. I recently came across a wonderfully lucid statement made by a black South African pastor, the Reverend M. S. Tladi, whose parish is in Soweto. He said that the Church's duty is to define general *principles* of political and social life, but to leave particular *applications* (my italics again) to politicians and individual Christian believers—to those with the expertise and local information to know what is appropriate and expedient.

D.C. At the time of a general election, I suggest to clergy that their role is to examine the aims and principles of the candidates, on which they base their political programmes, and see which approximate most closely to Christian insights. Then the people can be left to decide for themselves whom to vote for.

There are many issues about which a priest is not competent to judge, and so our task, as the African pastor suggests, is to clarify the principles on which society can healthily function.

Jesus Himself was not prone to giving a number of detailed commands. He pointed towards the ultimate direction, the Way of the Father, and left people to make their own spiritual journey.

110

R.D. In one of his essays, D. H. Lawrence wrote: 'I know the greatness of Christianity: it is a past greatness . . . The adventure is gone out of Christianity.' Some years later J. B. Phillips asked: 'How can we realise afresh the revolutionary character of Christianity's message?'

D.C. That is precisely what Phillips was trying to do when he translated the New Testament. 'The destruction that wasteth at noonday' (Psalm 91:6) afflicts a Church as ancient as ours. As someone once said: 'A groove is next to a grave.' We need to learn from a young Church, such as the one in Kenya; or from a Church, as in some South American countries, which has to contend with an inimical government.

R.D. In the early Sixties one of the Sunday newspapers published results of a large survey on religious belief. Among its findings was that most people thought the influence of the Church was much less than in the past, but at the same time many people wanted the Church to have more say in current events and to give a stronger lead in social matters and the importance of family life. I am sure that a similar poll now, twenty years later, would yield the same result.

D.C. I believe strongly that the Church should speak about current affairs clearly and directly; give a lead in social issues; and constantly stress the importance of family life—'whether they will hear, or whether they will forbear' (Ezek. 2:5).

I often wonder what these polls mean by 'the Church'. If you press them, they generally mean the Archbishop of Canterbury!

An Archbishop of Canterbury has to choose carefully which issues to comment on. He does best if he reserves his opinion for the right moment on the right issue. Sometimes he will give his views as representative of the Church; sometimes he will refer the questioner to, shall we say, the Board for Social Responsibility; and sometimes he will do some research on the issue and perhaps raise it in the House of Lords.

Archbishop Cyril Forster Garbett, who was at York from 1942 until his death in 1955, had an exceptional gift, not so much for saying something original but for keeping his finger on the pulse of national events. He was not intellectually brilliant like Temple, but was thoughtful and well-read. He expressed his views clearly and chose his moment well.

I sometimes say to people in the media who are putting questions to me: 'I happen to be in a position of leadership, but if you too are a committed Christian, then *you* are the Church, working for Christ.'

8 CHRISTIAN DOCTRINE

R.D. Are all aspects of Christian doctrine equally important to you? I imagine that in the fullness of time certain themes cling to you more resolutely, taxing you, challenging you.

D.C. Perhaps we question even more in older age than we did in our youth because we know that life and theology are much bigger than we once thought. It is vital to go on questing and searching.

Certain basic doctrines are continuingly meaningful to me: the divine initiative; the fact that God discloses His mind and will—as the Bible says, 'God speaks' (Heb. 1); the fact that God spoke, and still speaks, supremely in a Son; the fact that revelation is mediated to succeeding generations by the Holy Spirit in the Church. And you cannot, it seems to me, be a mature Christian thinker without having a framework of eschatology. Eschatology is 'the doctrine of last things', including subjects such as death, judgment and the Second Coming: subjects which, however much we think, talk and write about them, finally elude us.

To come back to your question 'Is one part of doctrine more important, more fundamental, to me than another?'—let me give you an illustration: the Virgin Birth of Christ is of far less importance to me than the Resurrection.

R.D. On the subject of the Virgin Birth, what is your own understanding, as a linguist, of the description of Mary given by St. Matthew (1:18–25) and St. Luke (1:26–38)?

D.C. The Hebrew Old Testament passage reads: 'a young woman shall conceive, and bear a son, and shall call his name Immanuel' (Isa. 7:14). The Hebrew *almah* means simply 'a marriageable young woman'. The Septuagint chose the word *parthenos*, a virgin. The New Testament, in following

113

the Septuagint, is thus more specific than the Old Testament and implies a status—virgin—not necessarily implied in the Hebrew.

R.D. In your book *The Christian Faith* you defined sin as 'the worship of anything, however good in itself, which detracts from worshipping God'. Do you still hold to that? I have a feeling that some of the younger generation want to wriggle away from any concept of sin.

D.C. This is partly the result of what I would call the third or fourth generation of semi-paganism in England, where the Ten Commandments are virtually unheard of, still less the holiness of God, or the possibility that God can be offended.

In addition, a misunderstanding of some schools of psychology leads people to think not in terms of sin but of unfortunate inherited factors or unfavourable early environment: an excuse to diminish personal responsibility and any concept of volitional rebellion against ultimate standards.

These two trends make it extremely hard for a preacher in the late twentieth century to convey what Christians mean by sin.

The Hebrew word *chata* is used, for example in Judges (20:16), for slinging a stone and 'not missing the mark'. If you haven't got a mark, a standard, a code of behaviour, to miss, then the very idea of missing is lost.

R.D. You have already touched on one of the great conundrums of history which taxes every generation and has probably done so since the beginning of mankind: that is the question of fate versus free will.

D.C. If you push the determinist viewpoint too far, man comes to be seen as little more than a helpless puppet. This seems to me to be contrary to the Christian doctrine of man as well as to the evidence all around us. I believe that man does have an element of freedom of choice.

R.D. What is meant by the grace of God?

D.C. This is one of the major Old and New Testament concepts. In Old Testament terms, the loving-kindness of

God is linked with the concept of a God who enters into a covenant relationship with people, Himself making the first move and inviting mankind to respond. We have many examples of this covenant relationship, such as those with Noah, Abraham and Moses.

In the New Testament this doctrine becomes greatly enriched. The simplest definition of the word *charis*, grace, is 'divine love in action', divine love manifesting itself in and through people.

What is particularly interesting is that *charis* is linked linguistically with the verb 'to forgive'. In the parable Jesus tells of the two debtors (Luke 7:41–3), the man to whom they owed a debt *graced* them both. All they could do was seek for the grace, the forgiveness, the loving-kindness, of the creditor. Here we have an illustration of how close are the teachings of Jesus and of Paul. *Charis* is a theme regnant in the Pauline writings.

R.D. If I were not a Christian, if I were a Moslem or a Hindu, I would be deeply puzzled by John 14:6: 'Jesus saith unto him, I am the way, the truth and the life; no man cometh unto the Father but by me.'

D.C. I too have found that passage difficult. In the Gospels—as in all great scripture—we will come across a *skandalon*, something we stumble over. We should not try to whittle down the meaning in an attempt to make scripture acceptable to everybody. To adapt the Latin *exit in mysterium*, all theology merges into mystery.

What I take this passage to mean is that 'only in and through the person and revelation of Christ will you come to know God in the *fullness of his Fatherhood*'. This avoids the interpretation that there can be no divine revelation except through Christianity; and it allows that God down the centuries has been manifesting aspects of Himself through faiths other than Christianity.

Many Christians would want to add their strongly-held belief that the glory and effulgence of the revelation of God is to be seen uniquely in the face of Jesus. For this reason, we

115

speak of Jesus as the incarnation of *the* Word, indeed He is the Word itself; and we note the importance of the great Christological passages—Colossians 1, Hebrews 1 and John 1. They illuminate Christ's nature and His life-work.

R.D.   In your book *The Heart of the Christian Faith* you said that all great theology evolves and merges into mystery. And elsewhere you quoted Cardinal Suhard's splendid injunction 'to keep the mystery of God present to men'. Please would you develop that idea.

D.C.   When our small, finite minds try to say something about infinity we are confronted by mystery. We are surrounded by mystery. 'Jesus', says St. John (13:3), 'knowing that . . . he was come from God, and went to God . . .' When you try to put that into human language—what it means to come from God and return to God—you surrender humbly to the mystery of God.

R.D.   In his book *God our Contemporary*, J. B. Phillips wrote: '. . . since a great many people know nothing of the Christian certainty of life beyond death, the power of death to inspire and terrify is restored to a pagan level . . . [and many adopt] a slightly cynical fatalism.' Later on he says: 'Where there is no belief in a purpose extending beyond this life, people are inevitably oppressed by a sense of futility.' I take him to be implying that to believe in an after-life gives us a unique and stronger sense of our worldly life.

D.C.   I am sure that is true. If you agree with Bertrand Russell that when you die, you rot, then your attitude not only to God but to your fellow human-beings is likely to be markedly different from what it is if you view men and women as temporary passengers on this earth, and permanently children of an eternal God.

What Phillips says about the fear of mortal death reminds me of a powerful passage in the Epistle to the Hebrews (2:15) about those 'who through fear of death were all their lifetime subject to bondage'. You are liberated from that if you believe in the Resurrection.

9 CHRISTIAN LIFE

R.D. Monica Furlong in her book *Travelling In* describes the religious person as 'one who believes that life is about making some kind of journey'.

D.C. I like that. It reminds me of something said by John Mackay of Princeton Theological Seminary: 'Truth is found not on the balcony but on the road.'

R.D. We were talking the other day about Leonard Wilson. While he was in prison and being tortured by the Japanese, they tried to force him to deny Christ and declare his hatred for them. He replied, 'I hate what you do but I don't hate you.' Is it possible to love everyone?

D.C. Wilson came very close to our Lord at that time. It was on the Cross that Jesus was able to say, 'Father, forgive them; for they know not what they do' (Luke 23:34).

I am sure it *is* possible to love someone whom you find it hard to like. *Eros* is primarily emotional love. *Philia* is loving-kindness. *Agape* is the deepest form of love, and Stephen Neill gives a profound definition of it: 'Love is the set of the will for the eternal welfare of another'.

There is, there should be, a large element of emotion in love, but the primary, the enduring, aspect is the volitional. Feelings may come and go, but *agape* endures (1 Cor. 13:7). Many people today fail to grasp this.

R.D. It is a great loss to the English language that we don't seem to have words that indicate the different aspects of love.

D.C. *Agape*, rarely used in pre-Christian times, is the dominant New Testament word for 'love'. A new ideal of love was born into the world in Bethlehem which needed a different word to express it. The old words, like old coins, had become worn and tarnished.

117

It is sad that the word 'charity' which in seventeenth-century English meant what you and I now mean by 'New Testament love'—a deep, solid, strong quality—is used for little else than the giving of money.

R.D.   In the great triad of responsibilities—love of God, of my fellow man, and of myself—the last is often under-rated or even neglected. There is a widespread fear that self-esteem might degenerate into inappropriate self-regard. We need to use and rejoice in our natural gifts and yet not flaunt them.

D.C.   I was talking about that to a group of clergy just the other day, reminding them of the dominical injunction: 'Thou shalt love thy neighbour as thyself.' I also read them a passage from a Lent Book *From Strength to Strength* which Mervyn Stockwood wrote when he was Bishop of Southwark. He said that a feature of Christ's healing is that it enables us to see ourselves as we truly are and to accept ourselves rather than be ashamed: 'It is only when we can love ourselves, warts and all, and not hate ourselves and feel guilty, that God can use us.'

Those words, and the meaning and intention behind them, can bring relief to many burdened people. An over-sensitive conscience is so terrifying a master that religion and life itself can become a burden which God never intended. Accept yourself as you are, and don't try to force yourself into another and idealised mould. This is not to lapse into self-indulgence, but to enter into a new freedom. It is significant that our Lord gave two affirmative commandments: 'Thou shalt love the Lord thy God' and 'Thou shalt love thy neighbour as thyself' (Matt. 22:37–39) in place of the ten of the Old Testament which were mostly prohibitions.

R.D.   There are some wonderful lines in Charles Wesley's hymn 'Forth in thy name, O Lord, I go'. I especially value his suggestion that one of the marks of a Christian is someone who maintains an '*even* joy'. What does that mean to you?

D.C.   That one should not identify too closely with success or failure, but remain steady in hope, in peace, and in joy. This is Christ's last legacy to His people: 'my peace I give unto you' (John 14:27).

R.D. Just as there is love deriving from will and love deriving from emotion, so also there is a joy that comes from feelings, one's senses, and from temporary conditions; there is also a quality of joy which comes from a disciplined and harmonious Christian life.

D.C. The peace of God protects and garrisons the heart so that false idols, false loves, cannot force their way in. Rainey, who was Principal of a Free Church theological college, said that 'joy is the flag flown from the citadel of the heart when Christ is in residence.'

But we must always remember that different people have different temperaments. Some people very rarely feel low and depressed; others go down to the depths and have to wait a long time before regaining a sense of joy in life. Their trouble is made worse if they say to themselves, 'My depression is a sign of failure of Christian discipleship. My faith should have rescued me.'

R.D. Chesterton once said, 'A saint is someone who knows he is a sinner.' Do we have to experience the absence of God before we can know His presence?

D.C. Most, if not all, the saints had periods when God seemed remote. Spiritual writer after spiritual writer describes the 'dark night of the soul'. The Psalms are full of pleadings: 'Hide not thy face from me; put not thy servant away in anger . . . leave me not' (Ps. 27:9); 'O my God, I cry in the daytime, but thou hearest not' (Ps. 22:2); 'Cast me not off in the time of old age' (Ps. 71:9).

R.D. Is this what present-day theologians mean by 'the agnosticism of real faith': the assertion that one cannot have a genuine faith without some measure of doubt?

D.C. Yes. I cannot imagine that any thoughtful Christian could honestly say, 'I have never had a doubt in my life'. I myself would accept the description 'a Christian agnostic' or 'a Christian humanist' if these are taken to mean that I have a series of deep questions about basic life issues which are not resolved just because I am a Christian.

'*Homo sum; humani nihil a me alienum puto*—I am a man; nothing that has to do with humanity do I consider to be foreign to me.' This was said by a Roman, Terence, in the second century B.C. It could equally well have been a quotation from one of the existentialists of this century—which shows that the concept of humanism is supra-temporal.

I am a human being, made in the image of God. 'Humanist' is a noble and glorious word. Let us not abandon it for use only of an agnostic or an atheist.

R.D. John Robinson in *The Difference in Being a Christian Today* wrote: '. . . the similarity between . . . Christians . . . and the best humanists is not, as it appears to so many churchmen, a threat, but a confirmation . . . For if Christianity is the truth about what it means to be human, then our aim should be to have more rather than less in common, and we should rejoice when we find a convergence.' There is a good example of your favourite 'both/and' approach.

D.C. That is a fine passage and must surely be the outcome of a strong belief in the incarnation. Saint Irenaeus said, 'Jesus Christ, because of His great love, was made as we are, in order that He might make us to be what He Himself is.' There is no part of me which God does not want to redeem, and there is no part of my manhood which Jesus did not take on at the Incarnation, sin apart.

R.D. Although the Christian and the humanist may both profess to love their fellow man, the Christian—it seems to me—has an extra dimension in his loving: he is enabled to love others because God first loves him.

D.C. The Christian sees in his fellow man something vital which the humanist doesn't see: that every person is a child of God destined for eternity. I come back to Stephen Neill's definition of love: seeking 'the *eternal* welfare of another'. That adjective is of great importance. I must therefore treat my fellow human-being not simply as someone I want to help to get the maximum pleasure from this life, but as a person destined for eternity, whose deepest character and soul is being moulded now.

R.D.   Your word 'mould' brings me back to the subject of personal doubt. A trap can be set for the priest as well as for the doctor. We come to them often with a strong need, spiritual or medical. When entrusting ourselves to their care and under-standing, we tend to project a certain almost superhuman strength onto them. This may trap them into not being able to share their doubts, and they may become unable to admit doubts even to themselves.

D.C.   I often tell clergy that the pulpit is not the place to express your doubts. A study is the place for this, or a study circle, in which fellow disciples can give strength to each other and discover the meaning and reality of the Church as a fellowship. I would, however, like to add a caveat to what I have just said about the pulpit. It can be a help to people who themselves are going through a time of struggle to know that faith is not an easy matter for the person in the pulpit. And so the sharing of the fact of one's inner wrestling—rather than the detail of it—can be a sympathetic gesture.

In the New Testament, especially in the Johannine literature, we find an emphasis on knowing; and yet we can see that these writers are grappling with vast issues of life and of faith. In Romans 8, 9, 10 and 11 we can almost hear Paul, like a bear in a net, trying to claw his way free.

Even in Romans 8, one of the most uplifting passages ever written and yet one which stretches us beyond human com-prehension, we are made aware of the immensity of the issues; but a 'know', an element of assurance, shines through. 'We know that in everything God works together for good with those who love him, who are called according to his purpose' (Rom. 8:28, RSV). A parallel is to be found in Philippians (2:12–13, RSV): '. . . work out your own salvation with fear and trembling; for God is at work in you, both to will and to work for his good pleasure'. Out of this quest for deeper understanding emerges the light of solid truth as Paul has experienced it.

Perhaps the best course for a preacher is to combine his own sense of questioning and doubting and awe with whatever degree of the Johannine and Pauline certainties he can affirm. This will bring relief and balance to the men and women in the pew.

R.D. What you have just said seems to link with the distinction Jesus made between what He shared with the multitudes and what He shared with His disciples in the upper room.

D.C. 'Unto you it is given to know the mysteries of the kingdom of God: but to others in parables' (Luke 8:10). Two classics of Bible scholarship have helped me on this subject: T. W. Manson's *The Teaching of Jesus*, and *The Central Message of the New Testament* by Joachim Jeremias.

There are those who have committed themselves to the Way of God, and to them the secrets of the Kingdom are disclosed as and when they are open to receive them. There are others who mock. A third group was described at the end of Acts 17 (verse 32) who said: 'We will hear thee again of this matter'. They procrastinate. They show mild interest. We shall always have a large penumbra of people who respond to the teaching in a shallow way. They may say to themselves, 'This is just one more philosophy' or 'What a good voice he has' or 'How good-looking he is'.

Weeds grow freely and try to crush a new plant. I have an idea that the parable of the sower—which would be more aptly named 'the parable of the different types of soil'—was autobiographical. What Jesus preached fell by the wayside like seed: some fell on very poor soil; some began to germinate but soon died; and some flourished. For this reason Jesus gave two strata of teaching.

R.D. In another parable it is not the dutiful son but the prodigal son for whom the fatted calf was killed. How can a Christian avoid the danger of self-righteousness?

D.C. The prodigal came back saying in effect, in the words of the hymn 'Rock of ages':

> Nothing in my hand I bring . . .
> Naked, come to thee for dress
> Helpless, look to thee for grace . . .

The older boy said, 'Look what I have done all this time. But what do I get for it?' You cannot justify yourself to God in that way. Only when you admit total dependence and surrender, only then can you receive the grace of God and be filled with Christ's love and all-giving.

This topic gives us yet another illustration of the brilliance of Paul as expositor of the teaching of Jesus. The whole thesis of good works versus faith, which Paul expounds at length in his letters, is a kind of exposition of the second half of Luke 15, the parable of the Prodigal Son, which it would be more correct to call the parable of the Two Lost Sons: the *roué* who crept back home disillusioned and in rags, with nothing to offer—all he could do was receive the grace and forgiveness of his father; and the older brother who had maintained a rather narrow credit-and-debit relationship with his father—'Lo, these many years do I serve thee, neither transgressed I at any time thy commandment' (Luke 15:29)—but couldn't begin to understand his father's real nature: love, freely given.

Temple once said that ultimately all one has to offer is the sin from which to be redeemed. The younger son had no idea that his father put a lamp in the window every night in the hope of his return. The younger son felt degraded, unclean and unworthy, almost to the point of suicide, but a flicker of hope caused him to say, 'I will arise and go to my father' (Luke 15:18); 'I will confess my weakness and ask to be allowed to start again.'

Real, deep faith has not the certainty of continuous possession. Real faith is, in essence, fragile. Real faith is the willingness to kneel down, with hands open and upturned, prepared to listen, ready to receive whatever God chooses to bestow.

R.D. What you have just said about the need to surrender to the will, love and grace of God, reminds me of one of my favourite passages from Bonhoeffer's *Letters and Papers from Prison*: 'To be a Christian does not mean to be religious in a particular way . . . but to be a man—not a type of man, but the man that Christ creates in us.'

D.C. I agree with that so much. What we are each given by God is a special mark of our particular brand of humanity. Here is a divine paradox: we yield to God all that we have, all that we are, all that we wish to be; and then our individuality is heightened and glorified by our discipleship.

God has reserved certain charismata especially for you. Cherish those charismata, and in that sense love yourself, because out of this material God is creating you as a man.

In those magnificent New Testament passages—Rom. 12, 1 Cor. 12 and Eph. 4:7–8—the word 'charismata' refers to personal gifts from the grace of God. He endows us with talents and abilities varying from administration to preaching and exhortation; from service to the showing of mercy. Charismata is a wide-embracing word for the riches God gives to His Church in the form of people as individuals.

I regret what is a very common misunderstanding of the charismatic movement, namely that the gifts of God's grace are confined to the more ecstatic qualities such as speaking in tongues. In fact, the gifts are almost beyond number in range and combination.

When we were in Canada we met a very old man who for years had been a dedicated follower of Jesus. His body had worn thin, but the soul had expanded with love. I sensed that the death transition would be minimal, so ready was his spirit for the next stage.

I was speaking the other day with Bishop Peter Ball about what St. Paul meant by 'he that raised up Christ from the dead shall also quicken your mortal bodies by his Spirit that dwelleth in you' (Rom. 8:11). I said to Peter, 'Do you believe this means precisely what it says, namely that a person who is living in contact with God can expect an accession of strength and vigour?' I ventured to add that in recent years I had come to believe in this probability, and that, in my own limited way, I experienced it in my years at Canterbury. Peter took this idea a stage further and suggested that, inasmuch as we grow nearer to God, our *spiritual* body is prepared for the next life.

10   SUFFERING

R.D.   In your book *The Prayers of the New Testament* you said about Easter: 'He took the blackest event of history and fashioned out of it His great design, and worked His sovereign will. The dreadful tragedy of man's sin became the vehicle of God's victory.' At the Cross, in our shared weakness and suffering, we find our true humanity.

D.C.   The problem of suffering does not necessarily become clearer as your concept of God becomes more refined. Indeed, if you conceive of God as Jesus did, as 'Abba', the problem of human suffering takes on a new immensity and darkness. He must be an insensitive person who is not often perplexed and sometimes almost defeated by this subject.

Years ago I was in Switzerland, in the most idyllic country-side where all Nature smiled. There I saw an old Swiss lady, her hands deformed and knotted with rheumatism. Although I have seen many worse examples of physical and mental suffering, I was struck by the contrast between this woman in pain and the charm and beauty of her surroundings.

The death of little children—from leukaemia, for example—makes you cry out, 'Why?' I am driven back, again and again, to the Cross and the Resurrection, one and indivisible, not for a clearly-defined answer, but for a clue, a torch which gives sufficient light to guide us, one step at a time.

R.D.   Many people outside the Church tend to pillory us because we can offer no clear answer to the perpetual problem of pain.

D.C.   Precisely because there *are* no clear answers. We can only walk in faith, and we have volumes of human experience—people who have been infinitely enriched by suffering. The God of the Resurrection takes the pain of human suffering and fashions out of it new love, new caring, new insights. And there on the Cross we see One who took upon Himself the burden of the world's evil and suffering and experienced it to the bitter end.

R.D.   Each Christmas I am moved by a line in 'Once in Royal David's City': 'Tears and smiles like us he knew'. The order of the words is surely significant: *tears* and smiles. I am immensely comforted that Christ has been through the mine-field of mortal life. This helps me to identify myself with Him who was mocked, betrayed, humiliated; and it reassures me that Christ can feel for me and with me in times of need.

D.C.   The Epistle to the Hebrews has been a constant strength to me. In chapter 5, verse 8, the writer says: '. . . though he were a Son, yet learned he obedience by the things which he suffered'. There is a Greek saying, a pun, *pathos mathos*— suffering is learning. The unique contribution of Christianity, in contrast to the Greek philosophers, is that the writers of the New Testament found 'suffering is learning' incarnated in a person and in His ministry. He continued to learn, to the very end of His life. Amid all our questioning about human pain and suffering, here is the heart of the Gospel: because of His first-hand experience, Christ understands.

R.D.   In *The Prayers of the New Testament* you wrote of Albert Schweitzer 'plunging into a veritable maelstrom of disease and darkness, and there he achieved an intensely affirm-ative attitude to life'. And Malcolm Muggeridge in *Something Beautiful for God* describes Mother Teresa's Home for the Dying, in Calcutta, as 'restful and serene'.

D.C.   I have visited one or two of her Homes in Calcutta and I met her once in Bangladesh: a tiny woman, owning little more than the clothes she was wearing, spending her life in the midst of appalling suffering and death, children rescued from dustbins, men and women found barely alive in the gutter, and there she either nursed them back to health or helped them with dignity into the next life. Like a refrain from her inner serenity, she kept using the words 'beauty' and 'beautiful'.

R.D. I can accept that suffering can teach us lessons we cannot learn in any other way, but is suffering always redemptive?

D.C. No, I don't think so. Pain and suffering, if experienced without the mediation of the Cross and the Resurrection, can lead to a life of anger and bitterness. At present I am reading a book by George Bennett who has done such valuable work at Crowhurst, near Hastings, at a home for divine healing. He gives example after example of people who have come to Crowhurst with a physical illness which is primarily a manifestation of inner unrest. Unchecked, this can lead to physical and mental breakdown—what one might call un-redeemed suffering. Bennett then goes on to tell how he sits quietly with these people, listening silently. Their stories and memories of woe tumble forth, marking the start of the healing process. Bennett comes back to the Cross as the focal point where light and en-light-enment are to be found.

R.D. Perhaps in our limited human way of thinking we separate suffering and joy, pain and peace, seeing them as opposites instead of as complementary.

D.C. The Christian experience does not by any means entail exemption from suffering. Indeed, as I said earlier, suffering is in some ways harder for a Christian because he trusts and has faith in a God of love. Only God in Christ at the Cross, reconciling the world to Himself, saves man from despair.

R.D. John Robinson in one of his books writes of the tension of being in the world but not of it. To what extent is suffering a spur to this: to be in the world and yet to transcend it?

D.C. We read in St. John (17:15): 'I pray not that thou shouldest take them out of the world, but that thou shouldest keep them from the evil.' I often think of Lancelot Andrewes as an example of someone 'in the world but not of it'.

My first interest in Andrewes is as a fellow Old Merchant Taylor. He was, in turn, Dean of Westminster, Bishop of Chichester, of Ely and of Winchester. He was notable as

128

an Anglican, as a linguist, and as a man of the Bible: he made a substantial contribution to the King James version of the Bible.

He was also a man of prayer and piety. He wrote his *Private Prayers*—a book he doubted would ever be published—while living much of his life in Court circles, at a time when—to put it as diplomatically as I can—the Court was not at its most spiritual.

Everybody in a public position faces this problem, whether he be a priest or a bishop or a lay person working in an office or a factory. But we do well to remember that tension helps to produce music: the violin string has to be taut. One end of the string represents your contact with the world; the other end, your contact with God. If you can keep your relation with God open and intimate and your relation with other people loving and compassionate, you will know and live the harmony of Christian discipleship.

11   PRIESTHOOD

R.D.   When a young person comes to you and says he wants to go into the Ministry of the Church, what qualities do you look for as marks of suitability?

D.C.   First I would look for a certain humility: a *sine qua non* in someone wanting to be a priest. He should not think he will be God's greatest gift to the Church; rather he should feel unworthy of the calling but have the hope that God in His goodness will look favourably upon him. Given genuine humility, anything can happen.

Then—and this is linked to my first criterion—I would look for at least the beginnings of a relationship with God in and through Jesus Christ.

I would look for someone who knows about *people*. This is vital. Academic knowledge is useful but will not suffice. A priest has to relate not only as preacher to congregation but as individual to individual, at points of deep need, intuitive of the longings of the soul. I often think of St. John's glorious description of our Lord: He 'needed not that any should testify of man: for he knew what was in man' (2:25).

Lastly, I would look for mental alertness. This may save him from staleness, the 'destruction that wasteth at noonday'. Noonday comes to some priests distressingly early: their preaching and teaching ministry then becomes dull, both to themselves and to other people.

To sum up: know yourself, know God, know people, and have no cobwebs in the upper storey!

R.D.   As well as those personal qualities, how important is administrative ability?

D.C.   It is a great asset if a priest can keep his desk clear, if he can guide committees, and if he has a sense of financial good housekeeping. Administration is valued as one of the gifts of the Spirit (Rom. 12:6–7 NEB; 1 Cor. 14:40 AV), but I wouldn't rate it anywhere near as vital as those personal qualities which I have just mentioned.

R.D. What are some of the pitfalls in the path for someone about to train for ordination?

D.C. One of the main dangers is to take for granted the miracle that you, who are 'less than the least of all saints' (Eph. 3:8), have been given the grace to be chosen. The priesthood is a miracle, a splendour, a divine adventure, which is renewed daily.

That phrase 'the least of all saints' is a comparative on top of a superlative. *Elachistos* means least; Paul adds a comparative to it to make *elachistoteros*—literally 'the more than the least of all the saints'. Paul creates this grammatical monstrosity to convey the glow, the awed surprise, which should characterise the work, life and attitude of a priest.

R.D. What else do you say to a group of ordinands?

D.C. One of the creative tensions many of them have to face is how to combine two major life-callings, marriage and the ministry, both in their early stages. The percentage of men in our theological colleges who are already married is far higher than in the past. That combination calls for wisdom and grace.

Another subject which ordinands usually want to discuss is how to achieve the right balance between study and activity. Some few are too steeped in books; others seem to have little inclination to read.

A high degree of personal integrity is necessary.

R.D. The Reverend Dr. R. T. Williams used to say to ordinands, 'Young men, beware of two things: money and women. If you go astray regarding either, remember this: God may forgive you but the people won't.'

D.C. That is well put. A priest should be 'holy, harmless, undefiled, separate from sinners'—as the Epistle to the Hebrews describes Christ (7:26)—while at the same time mixing with them as our Lord Himself did, with never a hint of scandal nor any suggestion of self-righteousness. He often seemed happier being with them than with the Pharisees.

The subject of money can be a subtle and tricky one. When I was a Diocesan Bishop and had dealings with the Church Commissioners, we did our best to keep salaries commensurate with the rise in prices.

We must guard the welfare of priests and their families, but there is a danger of the standards of the secular world—which gives priority to material wealth and possessions—invading the life of a priest, almost without his knowing it. The simplicity that is in Christ can so easily be forgotten.

R.D.   You spoke of the difficulty of combining marriage and the ministry, especially in the early years, but I am sure you would testify to the comfort and support you and your work receive from a loving wife and a secure marriage.

D.C.   Indispensable. I spoke a few weeks ago to someone who was contemplating the offer of a post of national importance. Looking back on my time at York and Canterbury, I said I couldn't have succeeded without a liberal dispensation of the grace of God; and a wife who shares my ministry and contributes so much. The deepest level of our sharing is in prayer together, both vocal and silent: this provides an irrigating and a fructifying element for my whole ministry.

R.D.   John Robinson has written of the priest's role as being 'a servant of the servants of God', but that may not be original Robinson.

D.C.   I don't know the origin of the phrase, but *servus servorum Dei* is often used of the Pope. This concept is grounded in Scripture, in the servant passages of Isaiah and in the ministry of Jesus. He 'made himself of no reputation, and took upon him the form of a servant, and was made in the likeness of men: and being found in fashion as a man, he humbled himself, and became obedient unto death, even the death of the cross' (Phil. 2:7–8).

That passage is at the heart of the doctrine of Christ's *kenosis*,

His self-emptying. If you take seriously the manhood of Christ, the Son of God—as the New Testament compels us to do—what does this dual nature imply and mean? This is a major theological and Christological issue.

In Hebrews (5:8) we read: '. . . though he were a Son, yet learned he obedience by the things which he suffered'. The growth of Jesus—as boy, adolescent, and young man—implies a development in knowledge; this, in turn, implies things yet to be learned.

As St. Bernard said of the Atonement: 'It was not the death, by itself, which pleased God, but the willingness to die'—in the years up to and culminating in the Crucifixion.

R.D. In your book *Convictions* you wrote: '. . . the value of many a clergyman's ministry—not all, by any means, but many—is in inverse proportion to the length of his entry in *Crockford's Clerical Directory*'. How do you justify that at a time when mobility is all?

D.C. Precisely because mobility is so widespread, society needs a core of people to provide, as it were, the firm centre of a moving circle.

When I hear of a priest who has spent no more than three or four years in any one parish, I ask myself why he is always on the move. Is there lack of depth? Is he impatient? How does he get on with other people? Has he ceased to be able to renew himself except by asking his Bishop to move him on?

By contrast, I think of a man such as Canon Peter Green (1871–1961), who turned down a number of bishoprics (he was offered Lincoln, Blackburn, Birmingham and New Guinea!) and continued to work amid the slums of Salford near Manchester. When the troops came back from the First World War, there was Peter Green to welcome them home. He would baptise a baby who, when grown-up, would bring the next generation to be baptised. Peter Green was the solid, stable core of an ever-moving society.

He was a voracious reader and a voluminous writer. For more than forty years he wrote a column for the *Manchester Guardian* under the byline 'Artifex', which means 'worker'.

Amazingly, he also found time to write nearly forty books. He was able to continue in one parish by virtue of his constant intake of mental and spiritual richness. But if you look up his name in an old edition of *Crockford's* you will not find a long entry.

R.D.   Also in *Convictions*, you say that parish priests 'do their best work if they are given a large measure of responsibility and are left room for the exercise of a large measure of individuality'.

D.C.   That was a verbal hit at any Bishop who interferes too often in the work of his clergy. A Bishop should assure his clergy that he is readily available to meet and talk with them, but they are men of God, men of character, and a Bishop should trust them and leave room for their own individuality to flourish. This will be enriching for both priest and parish; pastoral work is open to a variety of patterns.

R.D.   To what extent do the relatively small congregations of today inhibit priests from being individual and adventurous?

D.C.   This is where patience is needed. A priest ought to be a seer, a visionary; but a seer often has difficulty in conveying his vision to other people. He sees a truth, a possibility, a programme for his church, but his Parochial Church Council don't agree. What does he do? Does he lose patience? Does he become embittered? Or does he recall what was said of our Lord by Isaiah the prophet: 'A bruised reed shall he not break and smoking flax shall he not quench till he send forth judgment unto victory' (Matt. 12:20)? Perhaps the reed, blown over by the wind, can be coaxed back to life. Perhaps the smouldering wick can be made to give light again.

Has he got the resources, the inner endurance— *hypomonē*, one of the noble New Testament words—to accept the reservations of his P.C.C. and perhaps try again later? Grace and patience—these are the ingredients of an enlightened and effective ministry.

R.D.   How far are we really moving towards a priesthood of the laity, a priesthood of all believers?

D.C.   We have been learning a lot more about this in the last couple of decades, and it is an example of the way God can transform a difficulty into an advantage. The difficulty was not enough clergy. All the Churches suffered major losses of clergy and lay people during the two world wars and thereafter a decrease in ordinands.

We were forced to combine parishes and refashion boundaries. Many priests had several churches to look after. But God has a way of teaching His Church, often in unexpected ways. The slump in the ratio of clergy to laity has prompted the Church to recapture its vision of the laity as a worshipping and witnessing community.

Alongside our recruiting of an able and ample priesthood, we must continue to foster the use of lay people within the body corporate of the Church: in the Parish Eucharist, in the Reader movement, and in many other ways.

Men and women in our congregations who have teaching skills and whose hearts are filled with the grace of God should be given every encouragement. The Church will be enriched by their ministry.

R.D.   What role do you see, now and in the future, for a more specialised ministry, such as in pastoral counselling or religious broadcasting? Do you see this developing as an alternative to traditional parish work?

D.C.   I am a strong supporter of these variant types of ordained ministry but I hesitate over the word 'alternative'. For many years we have had chaplains in hospitals, prisons, schools and universities. Thanks to men such as Ted Wickham and Bishop Leslie Hunter, the work of industrial chaplains has broadened considerably.

Deep spiritual counselling is urgently needed in an age when so many people suffer from stress; but I don't see this as an alternative to the parochial ministry. That conviction has led me during recent years to call for more ordinands. I accept that the parochial system has to be rethought, especially for the conurbations where there can be as many as thirty thousand people or more in a parish. But I don't believe this gives us sufficient reason to abandon the ideal of a parochial ministry.

A man who can move freely among his people, to whom their homes are open, who can minister at baptism, marriage, sickness and death, and during the ups and downs of adolescence and middle age, in times of prosperity or relative poverty; a man of study and of the sacraments, a man of the Word, and a man of prayer—I still cannot conceive of a better or more privileged role than the ministry for such a man.

I therefore hope that, while we develop the specialist ministries, we shall continue to train first-class men for the whole-time parochial ministry.

R.D. Is the form of training ordinands changing enough with the times?

D.C. The pattern of training in our theological colleges has changed greatly since the days when I was a theological college Principal a quarter of a century ago. The danger now is that we try to cram in too much, too many subjects, and do none of them thoroughly. We don't go deeply enough into the basics such as Church history and Biblical and liturgical studies.

We should keep clearly in mind that theological college is only part-one of a training which will continue long after a man is ordained. More and more Bishops, and others who are responsible for the clergy, now see a greater need for post-ordination training. Because of this, parts of pre-ordination training can be reduced in scope, in the knowledge that they will be adequately covered later on, against a background of more understanding and more first-hand experience.

R.D. How would you describe the main changes in theological colleges during the last twenty or thirty years?

D.C. Teaching is less by lecture and more by group discussion. And there is less emphasis on languages. My predecessor as Principal of the London College of Divinity, if he was training a man for the London B.D., would provide courses in Latin, Greek and Hebrew. Many hours each week were devoted to linguistics.

For all my love of ancient languages, and for all my belief that they provide good discipline for the mind and excellent training for clear enunciation of what you believe and try to pass on to others—despite that, I believe the balance was wrong. I only hope we have not gone to the other extreme. Learing a language—preferably Greek, because this is the language of the New Testament—helps a man to get to the heart of a word, an idea, or a theological concept.

A major change in the organisation of college life is the greater participation of wives and of families who live within college grounds or very close by. In some of our colleges women are training full-time alongside their menfolk, intending to be parish workers, deaconesses, or teachers of religious knowledge in schools.

R.D.   In your book *On Preaching* you said that 'prophetic boldness involves loneliness and suffering' and in *Convictions* (presumably to newly ordained men) you said: 'Don't expect your ministry to be easy. On the contrary, you will often be misunderstood.' The loneliness which all leadership involves can be used to bring you into closer communion with God.

D.C.   I am sure that is true. Loneliness casts you back on to God the Comforter. A priest can and should share some of his problems with his Bishop or Archdeacon, but he cannot always be running to them.

A priest must bear the loneliness of a community leader and the loneliness of a prophet. A prophet must be prepared to say things which are unpopular and unfashionable. A prophet is exposed to much criticism as well as isolation. As you rightly said, this makes you more reliant on God whose Son knew about being 'alone . . . yet . . . not alone' (John 16:32) because the Father was with him.

R.D.   How widespread are problems of middle life for clergymen? I suspect that many clergy have difficulty in renewing their original commitment and in maintaining their freshness and ability to learn.

137

D.C. This is a very real problem. As well as what is nowadays called the 'male menopause', there is a danger that the early glow of being in the Ministry fades and you cease to marvel that God has called you.

Then there is the danger of the activism which kills spirituality: you become so busy and your diary becomes so full, and prayer is sacrificed on the altar of over-activity. The word 'hectic' should not be allowed into the vocabulary of any Christian.

Another danger is that a priest may cease to read. I often remind my clerical friends of the Bishop who was found in a priest's study, peering into the bookcase, and said: 'I was just looking to see when you died'. Mental and spiritual death can precede physical death by many years.

So often a priest suffers from a combination of these things: physical tiredness, over-activity, less prayer, little reading. But work and life go on, and he doesn't give himself time to stand back and reassess.

R.D. Did you ever as Bishop recommend to someone in this dilemma that he have a sabbatical period to rediscover the wellspring of his vocation?

D.C. We were wrestling with this whole problem in the diocese of Canterbury when I was there. A lot of rethinking is being given to the continued education and invigoration of clergy in mid-life. The ideal would be a sabbatical period, as of right, every six or seven years. But how can we finance this? And what arrangements do we make for his wife and children? In the meantime more and more priests—at times of need and *before* times of need—are being encouraged to go away for a few weeks, on retreat or for a course of study.

R.D. What are your reflections on Michael Wilson's suggestion that 'perhaps the greatest tension a priest must bear is the fact that he *openly* [my italics] stands for a God of love in a place of suffering'?

D.C. I can understand why you have stressed the word 'openly'. If a lay person's faith is shaken he can in a sense confine the expression of his suffering to his own immediate circle of family and friends. But suffering can have an extra-sharp edge for a priest, because Sunday by Sunday he has to go into the pulpit and preach about the God of love. If at times he can admit his uncertainty about certain areas of life, this sharing may strengthen the human bonds with his congregation. On many issues I am not ashamed to say that I am a Christian agnostic.

R.D. Only the true professional, in any calling, has the courage to say 'I don't know'.

D.C. Did Yehudi Menuhin ever talk with you about his periods of struggle to regain his technique?

R.D. Yes, he did. He had two major times of reassessment: one, I think, before his first marriage and one after. He suffered, paradoxically, because of the very facility of his early-flowering gifts; he had to make them his *own* in a new way.

D.C. Do you think he was a richer, deeper, more tender violinist for having gone through those periods of blackness?

R.D. Yes, I am certain he emerged both strengthened in character and with his whole musicianship enriched. Through suffering he undoubtedly gained in authority.

This leads me to want to talk with you about authority of another kind. One of the features of our times is that all authority figures are being questioned as never before. I am thinking not only of the priesthood but of judges, police, teachers, parents, managers in commerce, politicians.

One of the extra challenges which clergy are having to face is that many people in trouble say they would prefer to consult a doctor or a social worker or a psychotherapist.

D.C. I imagine that in some of the younger Churches, such as in Africa, you might find more reliance on the pastoral work of clergy. Here in England, as we have said, the mobility of the population prevents a long-term relationship with a parish priest.

Our first need is to have more men of real calibre in the

parochial ministry; then they must make themselves known and available. I think of a friend of mine who was a vicar in Hampstead, an area partly Jewish and partly Gentile. Three factors made his ministry effective. One was that he preached extremely well; his reputation for this soon spread. Second, there was good music so that people who went to his church experienced a quickening of their aesthetic sense. Third, it became known that anyone could go to him and unburden. He was understanding and he was never in a hurry.

There is no quick solution to your question. All we can do is gradually to select and train men of this quality, able to express their faith effectively and widely.

R.D. Are you concerned that some traditional aspects of a priest's work are being duplicated by other professions? For example, there are now twice as many full-time social workers as Church of England clergy.

D.C. That does not worry me. After all, every good thing comes from God. If I were a parish priest and knew of a social worker, a doctor, or a teacher to whom people were going for counselling, my response would be to thank God. If these men and women have charismata, gifts from God, this would be a cause for rejoicing. We each have a distinctive contribution to make.

From time to time I would help to arrange a meeting of such people—the local policeman, doctor, social worker, head-teacher—in their study or in mine, so that we could work together as a team. They would then know whom to refer to me; and I to them. The extent of human need is limitless. There is more than enough work for us all to do.

R.D. How great a problem is it that as you move up the hierarchy of, shall we say, the Anglican Church, the less time you are likely to have for pastoral work?

D.C. This is a real difficulty, and supremely so for the Archbishop of Canterbury. Nevertheless my staff knew that, however busy I was, a priest in difficulties was to be given first priority. My first care was for the clergy.

I also did what I could through those who shared responsibility for pastoral work: Suffragan Bishops, Archdeacons, Rural Deans.

R.D. A major problem in meeting pastoral needs is when a priest has to admit—to himself, to the person he is trying to help, or both—that he agrees with, say, the use of the pill or the remarriage in church of divorced people, but dare not say so in public.

D.C. Yes, this is a profound dilemma for clergy. At present it is generally understood that remarrying divorced people in church is not done within Anglicanism, at least not in England. Many clergy have to admit to those who come for guidance that they disagree with this ruling. Then they have to decide either to disobey the ruling or to say, 'All my sympathies are with you but I must be loyal to my Church.'

Within the Church of England certain Bishops have let it be known that they disagree with this ruling and hope to have it changed. The subject is very much *sub judice* at the moment.

A number of our Roman Catholic brethren hold an entirely different view on birth control from the teaching of their Church. I understand that many of their priests say to their people, 'Don't ask me. Do what you believe to be right.'

R.D. Lastly, perhaps we could talk about one form of priesthood of which the value is beyond many people's understanding. I should like to read you a short paragraph by Thomas Merton: 'In the eyes of our conformist society, the hermit is nothing but a failure—we have absolutely no use for him, no place for him. He is outside all our projects, plans, assemblies, movements . . . we are revolted by his insignificance, his poverty, his shabbiness, his total lack of status.'

D.C. When our eyes are eventually opened to ultimate truth, it will no doubt be revealed to us that the people of achievement cared little about status or honours but were devoted to prayer, meditation, the spiritual life: their commerce was commerce with God. 'But,' protests the man of the world, 'you can't prove that.' No, of course you can't. The mysteries of life are beyond proof.

The way of the hermit may seem mere folly; they represent a different, a unique, scale of values. But many people who would call themselves 'worldly' are beginning to be attracted by the vision. For example, people of all ages are intrigued by Bishop Peter Ball who is a monk. They know him as a man who owns nothing, who gets up in the early hours to pray, and so clearly lives the life of the Spirit. These people may not have read Matthew, Mark, Luke, or John; but, for them, Christian men and women of the calibre of Peter Ball represent the Fifth Gospel.

12 PRAYER

R.D.   You once told me that the most effective way to help people to learn to pray is to show them how Jesus prayed and 'help them to kneel down alongside Him'. From what we know of His life and Ministry, how did Jesus pray?

D.C.   First of all, there was a definite rhythm in the life of Jesus. He needed to withdraw from time to time: for example before the choosing of the Twelve He spent all night in prayer and communion with God. Rhythm is an integral part of Nature—in the tides, in the seasons, in the alternation of sleep and activity—and of the universe and of our relationship with God.

Second, Jesus taught us to begin our prayer 'Our Father'. Jeremias suggests that in no previous Jewish writing do we find a word of such endearing familiarity as 'Abba' used in dialogue with God. It seems that Jesus was readier to share this prayer secret with His disciples than when speaking to the multitudes.

We find this intimate way of seeking God reflected in Galatians; we find it also in Romans where this form of approach is clearly very precious to Paul—although he is writing in Greek he holds on to the Aramaic word 'Abba' because this was the word Jesus used.

The Father-Son relationship is the heart and basis of the prayer-life of Jesus.

Third, the prayers of Jesus show a deep knowledge and assimilation of Old Testament scriptures. His lamentation on the Cross—'My God, my God, why hast thou forsaken me?' (Matt. 27:46)—is a quotation from Psalm 22 (verse 1). 'Father, into thy hands I commend my spirit' (Luke 23:46)—again from His hour of extreme agony—is also Old Testament (Ps. 31:5). In His time of temptation in the wilderness and seeking divine aid, the Devil is three times answered by quotations from Deuteronomy.

In the Gospels we have illustrations of Jesus interrupting His work to send an 'arrow' prayer to God: 'I thank thee, O Father, Lord of heaven and earth, because thou hast hid these things from the wise and prudent and hast revealed them unto babes' (Matt. 11:25).

R.D.   Here is one of my favourite quotations about the nature of true prayer: 'How empty are our conceptions of Deity! We admit theoretically that God is good, omnipotent, infinite, and then we try to give information to this infinite Mind. We plead for unmerited pardon and for a liberal outpouring of benefactions. Are we really grateful for the good already received?' The unlikely source is Mary Baker Eddy's *Science and Health*.

D.C.   It is indeed a travesty of prayer to spend too much time informing God of what He already knows. But there are times when, like a child on a parent's knee, we need to sob out our troubles. This can be a first, cathartic stage of prayer, its purpose being to comfort ourselves in the presence of God rather than to impart information to God.

The Psalmists spent a lot of prayer-time offloading unhappiness and distress, almost to the point of blasphemy: not only telling God of their misery, caused by sickness or persecution, but upbraiding Him for slackness in responding.

R.D.   Mary Baker Eddy spoke of the importance of thankfulness in one's prayers.

D.C.   Especially if you are feeling low, gratitude in prayer will often lift your spirits. We are surrounded by wonderful gifts: they have all come from a lavish hand.

R.D.   One of the difficulties in my own prayer-life centres on the problem of time. God's sense of time and my sense of time, and what I long for, are often of a different scale.

D.C.   My own difficulty in prayer in relation to time is external pressure: the demands of the coming day or week distract me from my communion with God. The wrong thing to do when this happens is to get angry with yourself. The best course is to tell God more about the thought or worry that has come to you, interruptive though it may be of your set devotions. He understands.

R.D. The reverse of that particular problem is the very difficult art of waiting. So many people today, of all ages, are unemployed. Like Churchill in those wilderness years between the wars, they are waiting for a call.

D.C. I have never experienced the agony of feeling rejected, not needed by society, I have had times when I would have been glad of a move, but I cannot recall a time when I didn't have more than enough to do.

Throughout my ministry the daily offices for prayer and worship—whether in a college chapel or an episcopal chapel, at York or Lambeth or Canterbury—have been an enormous help to me. Regular prayer-times, set readings, intercessions for people in need—in the company of fellow Christians—can sustain you through the deepest crisis, giving rhythm in place of chaos, structure in place of uncertainty. Now in retirement the pattern is similar, but the call to prayer demands more from one's own inner discipline.

R.D. In your book *The Prayers of the New Testament* you mentioned the Psalms as being full of questions, and you said that this is one of the best forms of prayer.

D.C. The Psalms are replete not only with questions but with questioning, and with examples of man wrestling with the reality of God. Take, for example, the extraordinary passage in Psalm 78 (verses 66–67, Book of Common Prayer): 'So the Lord awaked as one out of sleep: and like a giant refreshed with wine. He smote his enemies in the hinder parts'. This is not blasphemous because it is so obviously sincere.

R.D. Your mention of sincerity reminds me of a radio talk given by Metropolitan Anthony in which he cited three basic ingredients of prayer: sincerity, reverence, and openness. He amplified the need for sincerity: not only in the time of prayer

145

itself but in being prepared to pay the cost, to accept responsibilities given by God, no matter how daunting.

D.C.   By openness, I am sure he means being open to the will of God: 'Then said I, Lo, I come . . . to do thy will, O God' (Heb. 10:7).

Reverence is manifest at the beginning of the Lord's Prayer: 'Our *Father* which art in heaven, *Hallowed* be thy name'. Here is a marvellous juxtaposition of intimacy and awe; the intimacy never becomes over-familiar. For this reason many people, myself included, place importance on the body's position in time of prayer: kneeling gives tangible expression to reverence. The body ought to express the mood and attitude of the soul.

R.D.   I would only add, by way of confession, that I often pray with two voices. With the fervent voice of prayer I may say, 'Oh God, I am an instrument in Thy hands', but at the same time my ego will get in the way: 'I think I know what is best for me. I know how I'd like things to turn out.' The way of prayer is beset with traps, some clearly visible, many subtle and hidden.

D.C.   *Corruptio optimi pessima*—the best things corrupted are the worst. Prayer is one of those 'best things'.

I am still just a beginner as a man of prayer. There is so much to learn and such a long way to go.

13 HARVEST YEARS

R.D. We began our conversations just after you left Canterbury. Your last few months there, leading up to that farewell Eucharist in the Cathedral, must have been very busy ones. What were some of the many practical things you had to attend to, for yourself and for the office of Archbishop, preparing it for the hand-over?

D.C. I wanted to leave things as neat and tidy as possible so that my successor wouldn't have too much difficulty in settling in. From a household point of view, Jean and I had to sell a lot of what we had needed through living in two large houses. It meant disposing of a great number of books because of our move to a new and much smaller home in a Kent village. This had to be done in a hurry due to the pressure of work during those last weeks; some of my books were at Lambeth and some were at Canterbury. I didn't have time to sort through them as carefully as I would have liked.

R.D. For how long did you and Jean have this house in mind for your retirement?

D.C. We bought it a couple of years before I retired. We are in a lovely part of Kent and within an hour's drive of Canterbury. Until we moved in, we were glad our house could be used by a local vicar. There is a friendly atmosphere about it: it has been lived in for four and a half centuries, as a pub, a tea-house, and a family home. My wife is adept at making a house into a home. We have already had many friends here, old and new.

R.D. I know that your retirement is very much a partnership.

D.C. Very much so, as indeed my whole ministry has been. One of the joys is that we can now have more time together. Jean enjoys having a comparatively small home instead of those large houses—what the Duke of Edinburgh once referred to as 'your tied cottages'.

Jean likes cooking and gardening. She comes with me on some of my travels. She has time to read more widely and is working on a book of her own. We both enjoy village life and see many of our neighbours, in their homes and in ours.

R.D.   And it is in this room, your study, that you do your writing.

D.C.   Yes, this was the tea-room. A carpenter has lined it with bookshelves for us and it is here that I do any serious work such as the writing of *The Name above all Names* and preparation for the typesetting of my book *Sure Foundation*.

R.D.   In your last few months at Canterbury, from the autumn of 1979 onwards, how clear a picture did you and Jean have of the outward form of your retirement?

D.C.   We had little time to think about it. Geoffrey Fisher was affectionately known, after his retirement, as 'the Curate of Trent'. I did not want to become the 'Curate of Sissinghurst', too firmly attached to one place. I wanted to be free to live a somewhat peripatetic ministry.

R.D.   Did you have any fixed points for your first year of retirement in the form of travel, holidays, or invitations to preach or lecture?

D.C.   We tried to keep the first few months relatively quiet. I was very tired and I wanted time to settle in, time to gain my second wind. In March 1980 I went to Atlanta, Georgia, and in April to Washington D.C., but these were my only engagements abroad during those early months.

Bishop Bennett Sims whom I had met during the Lambeth Conference invited me to take part in the consecration of his cathedral in Atlanta.

In Washington the College of Preachers was celebrating its fiftieth anniversary. I have had links with this College over the years and they asked me to give a few lectures to clergy who had studied there.

When I had time to set some priorities for my service in retirement I put very high the needs of the clergy. During the past couple of years I have devoted much time to lecturing and speaking informally to conferences and groups of clergy, here in England as well as in Uganda and North America. These are the people who have constantly to preach, teach, and give deeply of themselves. I feel very privileged to be invited to help teach the teachers and feed the feeders of the flock.

R.D. As you reflect on these recent contacts with clergy in various parts of the world, are there any particular themes or subjects which recur about their personal or professional life?

D.C. Many a time I have sensed a sincere gratitude by clergy when I have been enabled to say something about prayer or the Holy Spirit, or when I have been able to take a passage from the Bible and show its immediate relevance to their ministry, to the life they and their countrymen live, and to the issues facing all nations.

I often begin my time with a group of clergy by saying, 'You may wish to take notes. I shall give you a number of Biblical references because I hope my talk will be seen not as complete in itself but as a spark, an incentive, leading on to and merging with your thoughts and prayers in the coming weeks.'

I regard my contacts with clergy not as giving definitive 'This thou shalt believe' statements but rather as stimulation, encouragement, the sowing of seeds of faith and renewal.

R.D. I am so glad you have focused on the subject of prayer. So many issues tax us, both personally and universally, that one wonders if there is *any* solution apart from one world-wide appeal on a supra-natural level. All faiths and all generations are joining hands and beginning to speak with one voice.

D.C. So many of our young people have ventured towards Eastern mysticism, some seriously, some not sure of their direction but feeling the need of a wider dimension in their worship. We should have done more to teach them the fullness of Christian revelation and insight, and the mystics within our own tradition.

149

R.D. After you left Canterbury and had a few months to settle in, regain your energy, and collect your thoughts, how long did it take you to begin to see the shape of the months and years to come?

D.C. God is gracious and kindly: He allowed my sense of the future to emerge slowly. To some people, retirement feels like a bereavement. Retirement is a 'little death', it must be. It marks the closing of a great door of one's life, but God opens other doors and leads you through.

My main dilemma has been to decide what to do and what not to do. Many people here in England and in various parts of the world have kindly invited me to visit and talk and share experience. I try to keep a level of activity that maintains a balance between quantity and quality, and I keep time free for reading and writing. There is still so much to do: I have an *embarras de richesse spirituelle*.

Once a bishop, you are always a bishop, and from time to time I am asked to take services of confirmation. Last Sunday I preached in the Cathedral at Canterbury to the King's School; the previous Sunday I preached at another public school followed by discussion with the sixth form. Every such occasion is a privilege.

Silvanus Wani, Archbishop of Uganda, wrote and asked if I would lead a Quiet Day during the Provincial Assembly, their version of our General Synod. I decided to go, and to preface that special day with travel in Uganda, meeting as many people as possible.

In August 1981 I spent three weeks in Uganda. Thanks to President Obote's help and support, and by his providing us with a seven-man police guard fully-armed, I was able to visit communities which in recent years have seen few visitors. Archbishop Wani accompanied me.

Even though Amin is now gone, Uganda is still having a difficult time. I wouldn't have missed those three strenuous weeks for anything. I am so thankful that such an opportunity came my way. I'd been to Uganda in the mid-Fifties and also a few years later for their independence celebrations.

I had known this lovely country when it was prosperous. Now its people were full of fear. Most nights when in Kampala I heard what they call 'the music', a euphemism for gunfire. I was living in a house with the local Bishop, a house which for six years had had no tap water. And in the capital city I travelled over roads with potholes so deep as to bring a car almost to a full stop.

The faith and courage of Christians in Uganda are immense. They have lost their Archbishop, Janani Luwum, who was murdered, as were a host of clergy and lay people; and so Christians in Uganda today are sustained by recent martyrdom and loyal witness. Congregations are large and the Church is vigorous, ministering to the needs of its people spiritually and practically, a reassuring example of the power of the living Christ.

One day an African came up to me and said simply, 'Thank you for loving us.' Another man, in one of the most down-trodden areas, said that, through me, Jesus had visited them. That said much more about him than about me. I returned home both encouraged and humbled.

Some of their ways make us think again about our own values. I am the sort of person who likes to begin a meeting on time, but in many parts of Africa if a church service is due to begin at eleven and you don't begin until eleven-fifteen, no one seems to mind. I still believe in being punctual, as a sign of courtesy to others, but, in the West, sometimes the clock becomes a tyrant.

In Africa I saw the value of the extended family. Old people are part of their family for life, whereas we often send them to institutions where they may be well-cared-for physically but often desperately lonely. One of the privileges of living for a time in Uganda is to have large question-marks put on Western values.

Africans have an instinctive sense for colour and dance. Not far from where Archbishop Luwum is buried we had a very well attended service followed by an enormous feast. Then we were entertained by a memorable display of dancing. The earth resounded to their chants and their drums.

R.D. Did Africans bring out something new in you?

D.C. I felt a great freedom when meeting them: partly because I was there to minister to them; partly because they are suffering and this brings out the best that one can give. Most of the Christians I met have a simple, direct faith, very little theology. Spiritual depths are not necessarily intellectual.

They like you to leave every gathering with a gift. This creates problems because of weight restrictions on air travel, but I brought back a few treasures including a cowhide drum. I have it here in my study as a permanent link with those dear people.

R.D. Have new spiritual insights come to you in the last year or so?

D.C. Perhaps the way I learn best is when I am involved in a writing project. In trying to nourish readers and listeners, I too am nourished. The same applies to my travels. I learn much from the kindness, the warm reception, in Africa. In a different way I learn from the skill and efficiency of the Church in North America.

The vicar, or the rector as he is called over there, tends to be better provided for—in funds, in church organisation, in voluntary support—than we often are. But there is a danger in placing too much confidence in the well-managed mechanics of one's work. We should be guided by that wise adage in Zechariah (4:6): 'Not by might, nor by power, but by my spirit, saith the Lord of hosts.'

The late Bernard Pawley, our Archdeacon of Canterbury, on hearing that a diocese had installed a computer, said wryly: 'Now is our salvation nearer than when we first believed.' By itself, good organisation is like a Rolls-Royce without petrol.

Bernard was a remarkable Christian. He will live on in ecclesiastical history as having been 'our man in Rome'. He knew Pope John and was a close friend of Pope Paul. He did much to follow up the initial step taken by Geoffrey Fisher. Bernard's knowledge of theology and Latin, and of Italian which he learned in a prison camp, helped him to encourage

152

Anglican-Roman Catholic relationships. To the very end of his life, his droll sense of humour was perceptive but never barbed or bitter.

Once you are a priest or a bishop, you are always a priest or bishop. Your ordination, or consecration, does not cease when your retirement begins. The ministry, which you have done your best to fulfil down the years, you continue, in the mercy of God, in your retirement. This is after all only an extension of the basic premise of 'Once a Christian, always a Christian.'

In retirement the pace may be slower and you probably have fewer responsibilities but, please God, the ministry of being a Christian goes on. To think or do otherwise would be a dereliction not only of duty but of privilege. And even when one is no longer able to continue an active ministry—of preaching, teaching, celebrating the Eucharist, making pastoral visits—the ministry of prayer assumes new importance.

R.D. Does this presuppose a faith that God will find ways of using you in your retirement?

D.C. Until now he has been good enough to do so. As Newman says in his great hymn 'Lead, kindly Light':

> So long thy power hath blest me, sure it still
>   Will lead me on
> O'er moor and fen, o'er crag and torrent, till
>   The night is gone . . .

BIBLE REFERENCES

(Unless stated otherwise, all Biblical quotations are from the Authorised version.)

INDEX